CW0064185 9

PANZERS
IN THE SAND

Volume 1: 1935–1941

PANZERS IN THE SAND

The History of Panzer-Regiment 5

Volume 1: 1935–1941

Bernd Hartmann

Pen & Sword
MILITARY

Dedicated to the Soldiers of
Panzer-Regiment 5 **and** *Panzer-Abteilung 5.*

English Translation © 2010 by Battle Born Books and Consulting

First published in English in the United States of America by Stackpole Books in 2010

Published in Great Britain in this format in 2010 by
Pen & Sword Military
An imprint of
Pen & Sword Books Ltd
47 Church Street
Barnsley
South Yorkshire
S70 2AS

ISBN 978 1 84884 505 3

Pen & Sword Books Ltd incorporates the Imprints of Pen & Sword Aviation, Pen & Sword Family History, Pen & Sword Maritime, Pen & Sword Military, Wharncliffe Local History, Pen & Sword Select, Pen & Sword Military Classics, Leo Cooper, Remember When, Seaforth Publishing and Frontline Publishing

For a complete list of Pen & Sword titles please contact
PEN & SWORD BOOKS LIMITED
47 Church Street, Barnsley, South Yorkshire, S70 2AS, England
E-mail: enquiries@pen-and-sword.co.uk
Website: www.pen-and-sword.co.uk

CONTENTS

FOREWORD

After more than half a century since the end of the Second World War, the writing of the history of *Panzer-Regiment 5* and *Panzer-Abteilung 5* was a difficult undertaking, especially with regard to the detail in which it is presented. The author, who did not take part in the war, was compelled to study the sources in his work. Many gaps in the narrative and even contradictory statements made the work more difficult. Particularly unfortunate was the fact that the names of many members of the formations in leadership roles, such as battalion and company commanders, could not be determined completely. Despite those deficiencies, it was high time for the history of the regiment to be written, since all previous efforts at a comprehensive portrait had failed for one reason or another, and the only thing available were individual contributions or broad portrayals.

The time frame under discussion here was relatively short, but it was marked by important events that still influence us today. The soldiers of the regiment fulfilled their duties bravely and in a self-sacrificial way for our German fatherland. They fought in Poland, France and North Africa. Reconstituted as *Panzer-Abteilung 5*, they landed in the middle of the collapse of *Heeresgruppe Mitte* on the Eastern Front in the summer of 1944. Reconstituted anew, they were first committed on the Western Front, before they fought outside of Berlin and in Mecklenburg at the end of the war. The author made every effort to present events truthfully, since history is obligated to the truth. Consequently, the unfortunate and annoying tendency to load up any treatment of historical events with ideology—especially from the German viewpoint—is avoided. In addition, it was important not to observe the history of the oldest formation of the *Panzertruppe* in an isolated manner but to present it in the context of the war and military history.

This work is not intended to appeal just to veterans. Instead, it is designed to inform members of the younger generation about those times. Graphics are kept as simple as possible, with the aim of making the situation and conduct of the fighting understandable even to non-military professionals.

Bernd Hartmann, *Oberstleutnant a.D.*
Spokesman for the Veterans Association of Former
Panzer-Regiment 5

A Word of Introduction

Thanks to tremendous effort and a great deal of professionalism, the author has assembled a history of *Panzer-Regiment 5*—a regiment that led the way for the *Panzertruppe* in all of the theaters of war—that honors and memorializes all members of the regiment, the living and the dead. This book is a fitting tribute to my old regiment.

Werner Grün, *Major a.D.*
Former Battalion Commander in *Panzer-Regiment 5*

CHAPTER 1

Establishment of the *Panzertruppe* after World War I and the Formation of *Panzer-Regiment 5*

1. 1920–26: The Seeckt Era

The military defeat of the Germans in 1918 also meant the end of the numerically very small German armor branch, which consisted of only nine battalions, each with five tanks. Independently operating armored formations—a separate armored force—did not exist in the First World War.

The lack of a sufficient number of German armored vehicles contributed in part to the defeat of the German forces during that conflict, especially in the face of the masses of tanks employed on the Allied side.

According to Article 171 of the Treaty of Versailles, Germany was prohibited from having any "armored vehicles" or "any similar such materiel that could suit the purposes of war." Those provisions were monitored by an "Inter-Allied Control Commission" that was in force in Germany until February 1927.

In order to train for an armored force, which was vitally necessary in modern warfare, the German armed forces were reduced to using wheeled dummies that were pushed by soldiers or mounted on the chassis of light automobiles. The picture presented to the soldier on the ground by such displays was not well suited to conveying the elements of firepower, mobility and armor that defined the values of an armored vehicle or convincing them of the power and lethality of that new and modern type of weapons system.

From 1920 to 1926, *Generaloberst* Hans Seeckt was the Chief-of-Staff of the Army. Seeckt made the German Army into a gigantic school of leadership, which later proved itself immensely[1] and which attempted to do its bidding in the establishment of a modern army with special emphasis on technical proficiency and the mastery of weapons under the watchful eyes of the Inter-Allied Control Commission. Under Seeckt's authority, German soldiers and aviators received training on aircraft and fighting vehicles, under the strictest of secrecy, in the Soviet Union.

Following the disestablishment of the *Panzerwaffe* in the wake of the First World War, the tradition of combat vehicles was maintained in the *Kraftfahr-Abteilung* of the *Reichswehr*.[2] The motorized force consisted of seven battalions, which all reported to one of the seven divisions for mobilization purposes. The main mission of the battalion was to assure the flow of supplies for the divisions.

Supervisory responsibility for the motorized battalions fell to the *Inspektion der Kraftfahrtruppen*[3] in the Ministry of Defense.

---

1. Author's Note: Nehring, *Die Geschichte der deutschen Panzerwaffe*, 40. Hereafter referred to as Nehring.

2. Translator's Note: *Kraftfahr-Abteilung* = Motorized Battalion. *Reichswehr* = Federal Armed Forces.

3. Translator's Note: Inspectorate for Motorized Forces.

2. 1927–33: From "Motorized Forces" to "Motorized Combat Forces"

At the end of the 1920s, the Inspector General of the motorized forces at the time, *General der Artillerie* Vollard-Bockelberg, who has been called the "trailblazer for the *Panzertruppe*,"[4] gradually had the motorized battalion reorganized with motorcycle infantry companies and combat vehicle training companies (armored cars and dummy tanks). These would prove to be the nucleus of the future *Panzertruppe*. Thus, an increasingly motorized and combat-capable force evolved from what was once a transportation element.

In 1922, *Hauptmann* Guderian was transferred into the Motorized Forces Directorate from his light infantry battalion in Goslar. He was tasked with exploring the usage of motorized and armored forces and developed concepts for their employment, which later led to the idea of operational-level employment. He wrote in his memoirs:

> By studying military history, the exercises in England and our own experiences with our dummy tanks, I was reinforced in my belief that tanks were only capable of their best performance if the other branches, on whose help they always relied, were brought to the same status in terms of speed and cross-country mobility.
>
> In that formation, the tanks always had to play the most important role; the other branches had to orient on the tanks.
>
> One could not put the tanks in infantry divisions; instead, one had to establish armored divisions, in which all of the branches that the tanks needed to be combat effective were present.[5]

Thus, the development of modern armored forces was based on the concept of fast armored formations capable of large-scale actions at operational level, could accomplish missions independently and were capable of fighting as combined arms.

That concept became the basis for the command and control and doctrine of the *Panzertruppe* in the Second World War. It proved itself without reservation, and it still enjoys validity to this day in all modern armies. Guderian was the father of that concept.

After Guderian was promoted to *Oberstleutnant* in 1930 and assumed command of a motorized battalion, he returned to the Directorate of Motorized Forces on 1 October 1931 as its Chief-of-Staff. He reported to *Generalmajor* Oswald Lutz, who had been designated the head of the directorate on 1 April 1931. On 1 May 1933, the motorized battalions of the armed forces were redesignated as motorized combat battalions.

Both men complemented each other well, with Lutz eventually becoming known as the "father of army motorization" and Guderian as the "creator of the *Panzertruppe*."[6] One of Guderian's closest staff officers was *Major i.G.*[7] Walther K. Nehring, who was assigned there in January 1932.

After four years of hard work—often against the resistance of higher levels of command that were not prepared to accept armored vehicles as a separate branch—they created the prerequisites for the establishment of the first three armored divisions in October 1935.

---

4. Author's Note: Ritgen, *Die Schulen der Panzertruppe des Heeres*, 8. Hereafter referred to as Ritgen.

5. Author's Note: Guderian, *Erinnerungen eines Soldaten*, 18.

6. Author's Note: Nehring, 60.

7. Translator's Note: *im Generalstab* = General Staff. This suffix was appended after the rank of all officers accepted in the General Staff.

3. The Armored School at KAMA

Following negotiations with the Soviets, an armor school for German personnel was established with the code name of KAMA. It was located at a former artillery base with a gunnery range about five kilometers from the city of Kasan, about 750 kilometers east of Moscow. In addition, there was an aviation school at Lipezk and a gas-warfare school at Saratow.

Starting in 1928, the Soviet Union provided training lands, living quarters, equipment (including armored vehicles under development for the Soviets) and about 60 personnel. In return, Soviet officers were permitted to attend courses and exercises in Germany.

The instructors, engineers, technicians and course participants who went to the Soviet Union were temporarily discharged from the military for the duration of the courses. Soviets also attended courses at KAMA. In July 1929, the first prototypes of German armored vehicles arrived at the school, which still bore the code name of "agricultural tractors" to hide their true intent.[8] In addition to the training conducted, technical trials with the six heavy and four light "tractors" were given great emphasis.

The first course of instruction was given in 1929–30, followed by a second one from 1931 to 1932 and a third and final until September 1933. The school was dissolved in the fall of 1933, after German-Soviet relations worsened.

As a result of technical and tactical knowledge gained there, the approximately 30 officers who were trained there later formed the nucleus of the first German armored training units. The school had enabled the creation of the first batch of trainers and instructors, without which the rapid establishment of the first training formations in 1934–35 would not have been possible.[9]

8. Author's Note: The vehicles were produced by the firms of Krupp, Rheinmetall and Daimler-Benz.

9. Author's Note: Nehring, 45.

Many of those who attended or taught at the school were later to be found in leadership positions within *Panzer-Regiment 5*. Among them were *Major* Harpe (school director, 1932–33), *Hauptmann* Conze (tactics instructor), *Oberleutnant* Volckheim (tactics instructor), *Oberleutnant* Kühn (gunnery instructor), *Hauptmann* von Köppen (class advisor), *Oberleutnant* Thomale (course participant) and *Oberleutnant* Mildebrath (course participant).

As a result, the armor school in the Soviet Union yielded significant importance for the development of operational doctrine, exerted influence on the organizational basis for the establishment of the first German armored formations that followed soon thereafter and influenced the initial construction of German armored vehicles.

Another course participant was *Oberleutnant* Klaus Müller, who wrote of his experiences in May 1972 in an article entitled *So lebten und arbeiteten wir 1929 bis 1933 in KAMA*.[10] Here are some excerpts:

Second Part of the Course: 1931–1932

As usual, the technical preparatory work started in the middle of January. All of the tractors received new experimental tracks, with and without rubber pads. The heavy tractors also received track pins with grease. It was soon determined that the tracks with rubber pads encountered too much resistance when steering. The greased track pins did not work out at all, since water and sand entered through the pin gaskets, thus providing an extremely effective abrasive leading to premature wear. The desired larger roadwheels could not be mounted on these tractors.

The larger roadwheels, double sprockets for driving the track and open track with

10. Translator's Note: "Living and Working at KAMA from 1929 to 1933."

ungreased pins were therefore slated for future construction.

Starting on 10 May 1932, the German course participants started on their way home by land via Dünaburg and the frontier at Bigossowo . . .

Since the rations the previous year provided enough calories but lacked in vitamins, *Hauptmann* Conze arranged for seeds to come from Germany. As a result, the camp garden was able to provide considerably more fresh vegetables than previously . . .

In July 1932, *Oberstleutnant* Guderian visited so as to be able to form an opinion on further developments after taking rides in both the small tractors and the heavy ones. He dictated that the development of the heavy tractors was to be emphasized.

At about the end of July, additional tactical and technical training followed for the German participants. Gunnery aids consisting of sub-caliber devices, air guns and firing at film (gunnery movies) were tested. For the gunnery movies, *Hauptmann* von Köppen received instruction at the weapons directorate and at the *Ufa* studios in Neubabelsberg. In addition, improved firing devices were tested, which could be operated mechanically or electrically by the foot or the knee. There was an assortment of periscopes, sighting devices and different types of ammunition. The advantages and disadvantages of mechanical or electrical turret traversing mechanisms had to be determined, as well as sucking out or blowing out remaining gunpowder fumes. Since communications between and among members of the crew had to function without question, it was necessary to procure our own intercom system. There were difficulties in transmission from the non-moveable

part to the moveable part, the turret. The construction of the collector ring was no easy matter . . .

In the middle of August, the Russian course participants—some 100 commanders from all branches, as well as Red Army engineers—arrived. They remained until the middle of October. The Russian participants arrived without rank insignia, just as they had the previous year, so no one know who they were dealing with. All of the course participants were inquisitive and industrious. They placed special value on having a template for every type of order, which, it should be mentioned, could lead to a certain degree of rigidity. Camaraderie between the German and Russian participants was advanced by a weekly meal taken together . . .

The degree to which solidarity was fostered with the Russian forces is demonstrated by the invitation of all of the German course participants to a company function by the training company of the armor school in Leningrad. The political advisor of the company had issued the invitation and directed the evening affair, with the company commander practically functioning as a guest. When the Germans appeared, the Russians stood up, followed by a cheer that was given three times . . . despite beer and a lot of vodka, there were no drunk soldiers. The discipline was good.

We noticed whenever the Russians conducted combat gunnery that the targets were more lifelike than the ones we used, for example, Polish or Czech uniforms were portrayed. Russian exercises were also conducted with amphibious tanks, whereby an engineer company participated. The gunnery training continued. The ranges had to be laid out; there were no plans. Since there were no barriers, warning devices or telephone bunkers, the range safety duties had to be carried out by cavalry. The Russian translator was clear and simple: "Whenever it's booming, everyone goes away; they know, after all, that it's a gunnery range here."

Once a *Panje* cart[11] was hit by an armor-piercing round; the horse was able to escape!

Somewhat more awkward was the occasion when a Söda machine gun was being loaded—which had to be done at maximum elevation—and the Russian course participant accidently stepped on the foot trigger and placidly emptied both magazines with a total of 1,000 rounds. In a neighboring factory, one worker was hit in the shoulder, another in the upper thigh. How the matter was handled remained a mystery . . .

Besides *General* Lutz and *Oberstleutnant* Guderian, *General* von Hammerstein-Equord[12] visited us for a short while that year. Even if all of the higher-ranking officers traveled in civilian clothes and used code names, the actual secrecy as a practical matter was somewhat different. Whenever groups—always of the same size—always traveled from the Berlin-Zoo station at certain times of the year and always had additional baggage with them—all the same size and all numbered consecutively—then the rail officials and baggage handlers smiled in a friendly manner, wished them a good journey and a quick return. It was a bit stickier for a course participant whenever a wife, who was spending the time with relatives in a smaller town, was regularly visited by a

11. Note: A simple horse-drawn cart, usually with two wheels and drawn by a single horse.

12. Author's Note: Von Hammerstein-Equord was the Army Chief-of-Staff from 1931 to 1934.

Herr Schulz from Berlin with a payroll and the husband had completely disappeared from the picture. In another case, people were upset when a wife gave birth to a son shortly after the husband's departure, and he had apparently left her in the lurch. The same people were even more amazed when the husband reappeared half a year later . . . In summary, 1932 must be considered a year of considerable progress in training and cooperation with the Russians.

1933 Course

As a result of the political changes in Germany, we no longer counted on a detail of participants from the Russians, which was, in fact, what happened. As a result, the training of the German participants could continue as planned without any interruption. Extensive driving exercises alternated with live-fire exercises with machine guns or 3.7-centimeter cannon, even though the gunnery range was not often made available as a result of the worsening of relationships . . . In addition, there were no more exercises with Russian forces. In the middle of the intensive training came the news that the training and testing base of KAMA was to be closed by 15 September.

The preparations for the departure started in the middle of August . . . what, whether and how everything would be brought back was left to the clear directives of *Major* Harpe, who certainly had no easy time of it in negotiating. In a cooperative effort involving all of the Germans and the Russian employees, all of the weapons, ammunition, tanks—tractors, that is—and military equipment, as well as the library, were removed. Everything had to be packed in crates and sealed. The crates for the tanks

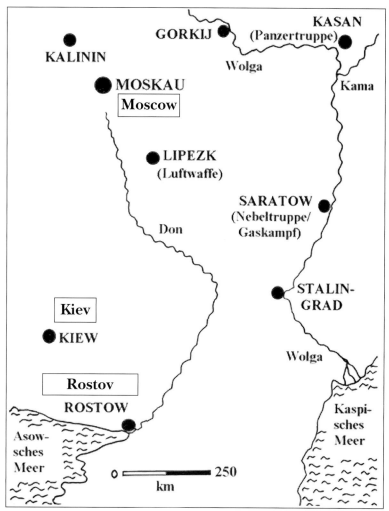

German Training Sites and Schools in the Soviet Union,
1922–33

had to be enlarged, since the vehicles had taken on other dimensions in the meantime. Special lifting devices had to be fabricated for the transfer in Leningrad. Everything had to get to the railhead at Kasan under its own power or towed. The freight cars that arrived had to be thoroughly inspected and greased for the 14-day trip to Leningrad, since none of the axles could be allowed to overheat during the trip . . . The equipment was taken under Russian guard on two trains to Leningrad. The movements all took place without incident, including Leningrad. The relationships with the Russian leadership were proper and irreproachable to the very end. In the meantime, all of the Germans had either departed from Kasan by train via Moscow or by ship via Leningrad. The last one to leave the camp was *Major* Harpe. Our leaving was not easy for the Russian workers. The initial period in the rebirth of the *Panzertruppe* was ended.

4. 1933–34: Establishment of the "Motorization Training Command"

The military and political situation in Germany changed fundamentally in 1933, when Adolf Hitler became the *Reich* Chancellor. Hitler recognized the operational possibilities of modern weapons systems, especially the importance of the new *Panzertruppe.*

The first formation of the fledgling *Panzertruppe* was established at Zossen, about 40 kilometers south of Berlin, on 1 November 1933. It consisted of officers who had attended the KAMA course and personnel details of around 50 men in all from the seven motorized battalions to serve as cadre and trainees.

For reasons of secrecy and deception, the new formation was referred to as *Kraftfahrlehrkommando Zossen.*[13] It initially consisted of a headquarters—commanded by *Major* Harpe and based temporarily in Berlin-Moabit—and a company disguised as a "Training Section" under the command of *Hauptmann* Conze. The new command reported directly to the Inspectorate of Motorized forces at the Ministry of Defense.

Duty Positions of the Motorization Training Command Zossen (as of 1 November 1933)

Commander: *Major* Harpe
Adjutant: *Oberleutnant* Martin
Staff Captain: *Hauptmann* Baumgart
1. Kompanie ("Training Section"): *Hauptmann* Conze
Officers: *Hauptmann* Thomale, *Oberleutnant* Köhn, *Oberleutnant* Ebert, *Oberleutnant* Henning and *Oberleutnant* Mildebrath

Officers in the Photograph on the Next Page with a Special Connection to *Panzer-Regiment 5*

1. *Generalleutnant* Lutz, the "Father of Army Motorization." Inspector General of Motorized Forces. Final rank: *General der Panzertruppen.*

2. *Oberst i.G.* Guderian, the "Creator of the *Panzertruppe.*" Chief-of-Staff of the Inspectorate of Motorized Forces in the Ministry of Defense. Last rank: *Generaloberst.*

3. *Major i.G.* Nehring, operations officer in the Inspectorate of Motorized Forces. From 13 October 1937 until July 1939, he was the commander of *Panzer-Regiment 5* (*Oberst*). Last rank: *General der Panzertruppen.*

4. *Major* Harpe, last commander of the KAMA Armor School. Effective 1 November 1933: Commander of the Motorization Training Command Zossen. Last rank: *Generaloberst.*

5. *Hauptmann* Conze. Effective 1 November 1933, the commander of the 1st Company ("Training Section") of the Motorization Training Command Zossen. Acting commander of *Panzer-Regiment 5* during the campaign in Poland. Last rank: *Generalmajor.*

6. *Hauptmann* Thomale. Effective 1 March 1934, commander of the 2nd Company ("Training Section") of the Motorization Training Command Zossen. Last rank: *Generalleutnant.*

7. *Major* Breith. Effective 1 August 1934, commander of the 2nd Battalion of the Motorization Training Command Zossen. Commander of the II./*Panzer-Regiment 5*[14] until 1938. Last rank: *General der Panzertruppen.*

8. *Oberleutnant* Mildebrath. Effective 1 August 1934, commander of the 6th Company of the Motorization Training Command Zossen. Battalion commander in Africa and occasionally entrusted with acting command of the regiment. Last rank: *Oberst.*

9. *Hauptmann* Köhn. Effective 15 October 1935, commander of the 1st Company of *Panzer-Regiment 5.* Commander of the II./*Panzer-Regiment 5* in Africa as a *Major.* Last rank: *Oberst.*

---

13. Translator's Note: Motorization Training Command Zossen.

14. Translator's Note: Roman numerals in front of the regimental designation indicate the number of the battalion; Arabic numerals indicate the company of the regiment. Line companies of combat regiments were numbered consecutively. Headquarters companies were not numbered.

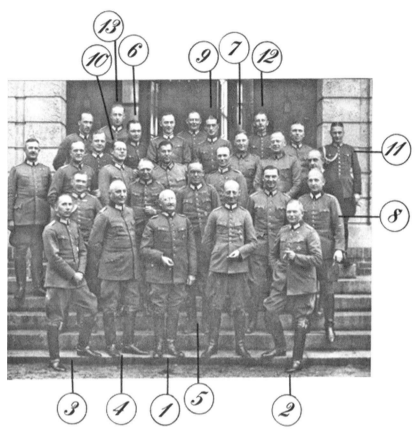

The founders of the *Panzertruppe,*
Zossen, November 1933.

10. *Oberleutnant* von Wilcke. Effective 1 October 1936, commander of the 2nd Company of *Panzer-Regiment 5* as a *Hauptmann.* As a *Major,* commander of the *II./Panzer-Regiment 5* effective 10 November 1938. Last rank: *Oberst.*

11. *Oberleutnant* Martin. Effective 1 October 1936, adjutant to the commander of the Motorization Training Command Zossen. As a *Hauptmann,* commander of the 5th Company of *Panzer-Regiment 5.* As an *Oberstleutnant,* commander of the *II./Panzer-Regiment 5* in Africa. Mortally wounded on 27 May 1942.

12. *Oberleutnant* Ebert. Effective 1 November 1933, commander of the 1st Company ("Training Section") of the Motorization Training Command Zossen. Last rank: *Oberstleutnant.*

13. *Oberleutnant* Henning. Effective 1 November 1933, assigned to the 1st Company ("Training Section") of the Motorization Training Command Zossen. Assigned as a company officer to the 8th Company of *Panzer-Regiment 5* until 1938.

Most of the military facilities at Zossen were constructed in the period from 1910 to 1913 to serve the forces training at the Zossen Training Area. The base camp was located at the western edge of the training area. Range II was only 1,000 meters away; Range III, 500.

During World War I, forces were activated at the garrison, which later saw action in the conflict. In 1919, several elements of differing free corps were billeted at the garrison.

From 1925 to 1929, portions of the buildings were used as children's recreational facilities for the city of Berlin. On 1 November 1933, the Motorization Training Command was established in the garrison.

In accordance with directives from the General Staff of the Army on 14 September 1936, Zossen was to be expanded to become the Headquarters for the High Command of the Army.

From 1937 to 1940, Camp "Zeppelin" was constructed, consisting of two bunker complexes, "Maybach I" and "Maybach II." Communications Center "Zeppelin" was also constructed to support the facilities. On 26 August 1939, the German Army Headquarters moved to Zossen and occupied "Maybach I," among other facilities.

Just before the end of the war in 1945, the High Command of the Armed Forces moved to Zossen, occupying "Maybach II." As the result of an Allied bombing raid on 15 March 1945, large portions of the main garrison were destroyed.

The town of Zossen was approximately 3 kilometers distant from the military facilities. The ranges for the garrison were located just east of the main buildings.

In the winter of 1933–34, the emphasis for training was placed on driver's training for the future unit activations. The hilly terrain associated with the

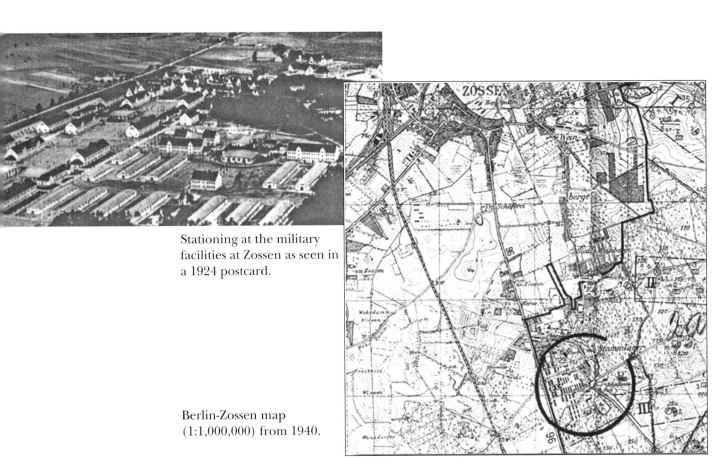

Stationing at the military facilities at Zossen as seen in a 1924 postcard.

Berlin-Zossen map (1:1,000,000) from 1940.

Chassis of a *Panzer I* used for driver's training at the Zossen Training Area.

Zossen Training Area placed great demands on the driving skills of students, who referred to the area as the "waves of the Danube." During this period, the first chassis of what was to become the *Panzer I* arrived for driver's training. As a deception measure, the vehicles were referred to as "agricultural tractors."[15]

On 1 March 1934, the Motorization Training Command Zossen was expanded to three companies. On 1 April, the headquarters of the command moved from Berlin-Moabit to Zossen. Effective 16 April 1934, a fourth company was added.

Command Positions of Motorization Training Command Zossen (as of 1 April 1934)[16]

Commander: *Major* Harpe (formerly the commander of the KAMA Armor School)

1st Company: *Hauptmann* Conze (formerly an instructor at the KAMA Armor school)

2nd Company: *Hauptmann* Thomale (formerly an instructor at the KAMA Armor school)

3rd Company: *Hauptmann* von Köppen (formerly an instructor at the KAMA Armor school)

4th Company: (16 April 1934): *Hauptmann* Wendenburg

In April 1934, the entire strength of the command, after the addition of 150 recruits, was 500.

On 1 June 1934, the Inspectorate of Motorized Forces was redesignated as the Motorized Combat Forces Command. *Generalleutnant* Lutz was simul–taneously given permission to establish a second Motorization Training Command. The second command was established through personnel levies against the first command at Zossen, from assorted motorized battalions and from several deactivated cavalry regiments. The new command was designated as the Motorization Training Command Ohrdruf. That was the first "fusion" of the command at Zossen, which was the nucleus for the establishment later on of *Panzer-Regiment 5*. More were to follow.

15. Translator's Note: In German, *Landwirtschaftlicher Schlepper* (*La.S.*).

16. Author's Note: Kampe, *Wünsdorf*, 24.

Starting on 1 August 1934, the training command at Zossen was expanded with personnel levies from *Reiter-Regiment 3* and *Reiter-Regiment 8*,[17] as well as three motorized battalions (3, 5 and 6). This enlarged the command to two battalions. On 1 October 1934, the command positions were occupied as shown below.

Motorization Training Command Zossen
Command Positions
Commander: *Oberstleutnant* Zuckertort

1st Battalion ("Zossen I")[18]
Commander: *Oberstleutnant* Harpe
1st Company: *Hauptmann* Thomale
2nd Company: *Hauptmann* Volckheim
3rd Company: *Hauptmann* Schwenck
4th Company: ?

2nd Battalion ("Zossen II")
Commander: *Major* Breith
5th Company: *Oberleutnant* von Heinemann
6th Company: *Oberleutnant* Mildebrath
7th Company: ?
8th Company: ?

On 1 October, the Zossen command was re-designated as *Kampfwagenregiment 1* and the Ohrdruf command as *Kampfwagenregiment 2*.[19] Both regiments initially kept their code names.

Both of those regiments, as well as the newly formed *Kampfwagenregiment 3*, that had been created out of *Reiter-Regiment 12*, were attached to Motorization Training Headquarters Berlin on the same date. All three elements were amalgamated into Fighting Vehicle Brigade Berlin,[20] with the first commander being *Generalmajor* Fessmann.

After serial production of the *Panzer I* was initiated in July 1934, the vehicle was delivered to all of the units, with the result that training could be started at the platoon and company level. The first company inspection took place in the spring of 1935.

The term "armored fighting vehicle" (*Panzerkampfwagen*) represented a combination of "armored vehicle" (*Panzerwagen*) and "fighting vehicle" (*Kampfwagen*). What that encompassed was a fully tracked armored vehicle with a main weapon, which is incorporated into a 360-degree traversable turret. For this work, the commonly used term "tank" will be used as shorthand for armored fighting vehicle.

Approximately 1,500 *Panzer I's* were built by the firms involved in their construction from 1934 to 1939.

With an effective date of 12 November 1934,[21] special-purpose clothing was authorized for service on armored vehicles. It was designed to replaced the previous special-purpose uniform worn by the motorized forces. The branch-of-service color chosen for the new branch was rose pink.

The branch-of-service color appeared along the edge of the jacket collar (later discarded), around the collar patches, on the shoulder straps (enlisted personnel) and as underlay on the boards (officers). The crash helmet/beret had only national insignia on it, but the field cap for both officers and enlisted, whether in field gray or black, had branch-of-service piping on it as well (also later officially discarded).

Initially, both the field jacket and the crash helmet/beret combination had no national insignia. Effective 11 November 1935, the national insignia started to be worn on both items.[22]

---

17. Translator's Note: 3rd and 8th Mounted Regiments (horse cavalry).

18. Author's Note: Both battalions also had a light tank platoon and a signals platoon.

19. Translator's Note: 1st and 2nd Fighting Vehicle Regiments.

20. Translator's Note: *Kampflehrstab Berlin* and *Kampfwagenbrigade Berlin*.

21. Author's Note: *Heeresmitteilung 34, Nummer 85*.

22. Author's Note: Referenced dates come from Schlicht and Angolia, *Die deutsche Wehrmacht*, 137 and 144.

	Panzerkampfwagen I (Sd.Kfz. 101) Model A In troop service starting in 1934	*Panzerkampfwagen I* (Sd.Kfz. 101) Model B In troop service starting in 1935
Identifying features		
	4 Roadwheels Low-placed idler wheel 3 return rollers	5 Roadwheels Idler wheel higher up 4 return rollers
Technical Data		
Length	4.02 meters	4.42 meters
Width	1.06 meter	2.06 meters
Height	1.72 meters	1.72 meters
Combat weight	5.4 tons	6 tons
Horsepower	57	100
Maximum Speed: Road	37 kilometers an hour	40 kilometers an hour
Fuel consumption (per 100 kilometers)	100 liters	103 liters
Crew	2	2
Armament	2 7.92-millimeter machine guns	2 7.92-millimeter machine guns
Armor plating		
Front slope, sides & rear	1.3 centimeters	1.3 centimeters
Upper and lower hull	.6 centimeters	.6 centimeters
Turret (upper portion)	.8 centimeters	.8 centimeters

Shown above is the special-purpose tanker's uniform in a period post card. This soldier was assigned to *Panzer-Regiment 6*, as indicated by the numerals on the shoulder straps. Members of other tank regiments wore analogous numerals.

The new uniform, consisting of black jacket and trousers, a dark-gray tricot shirt and black tie was chosen because it was not likely to show stains through oil and grease. It was also designed so that there were few areas that could get caught in the narrow confines of an armored vehicle. The crash helmet/beret combination, which was never really popular with the crews, was only worn until around 1940, when it was replaced with a black overseas cap.

A contemporary book on uniforms written by Eberhard Hettler in 1939 introduced the special-purpose tanker uniform by means of the illustration on the following page.[23]

23. Author's Note: Hettler, *Uniformen der deutschen Wehrmacht*, 49.

Special-Purpose Clothing of the *Panzertruppe*

For service in armored vehicles, personnel in the *Panzertruppe* and those issued armored vehicles will wear special-purpose clothing made out of black cloth: protective headgear, field jacket and field trousers.

Protective Headgear: The national insignia on the protective headgear corresponds to that worn on the field cap, that is, it is made out of silver-gray cotton for noncommissioned officers and enlisted personnel and light aluminum weave for officers. The oak-leave wreath for enlisted personnel, noncommissioned officers and officers is made out of silver-gray cotton.

Field Jacket: Basic cloth is black; piping on the collar and around the collar patches in the branch-of-service piping; collar patches in black with aluminum death heads. Shoulder straps with piping in branch-of-service color with the base cloth in black. Shoulder straps for noncommissioned officers with corresponding silver trim; officers use the shoulder boards of the field blouse. Insignia for enlisted personnel and musicians the same as the field blouse. No silver trim around the collar for noncommissioned officers, but twin rings for company sergeants. National insignia for all ranks out of woven silver-gray cotton on a black base.

Black field trousers without piping.

Worn with the black special-purpose clothing is a belt without sidearm. For parades, officers wear a belt with *four de guerre*. Noncommissioned officers and enlisted personnel wear the marksmanship lanyard, if awarded.

Footgear: Light lace-up shoes.

Sonderbekleidung der Panzertruppen

Zum Dienst mit Panzerwagen wird von den Panzertruppen und den sonstigen mit gepanzerten Fahrzeugen ausgestatteten Truppen eine Sonderbekleidung aus schwarzem Tuch: Schutzmütze, Feldjacke und Feldhose getragen.

Schutzmütze:

Das Hoheitsabzeichen zur Schutzmütze entspricht dem der Feldmütze, ist also für Unteroffiziere und Mannschaften aus silbergrauem Baumwollgarn, für Offiziere aus hellem

Aluminiumgespinst. Eichenlaubkranz für Mannschaften, Unteroffiziere und Offiziere aus silbergrauem Baumwollgarn.

Feldjacke:

Grundtuch schwarz; Vorstöße am Kragen und um die Kragenpatten in Waffenfarbe; Kragenpatten schwarz mit Totenkopf aus Aluminium. Schulterklappen mit Vorstößen in der Waffenfarbe, Grundtuch schwarz. Schulterklappen für Unteroffiziere mit entsprechendem

Treffenbesatz usw., für Offiziere Schulterstücke der Feldbluse. Abzeichen für Mannschaftsdienstgrade, Spielleute, Musiker wie zur Feldbluse. Keine Kragentreffen für Unteroffiziere, jedoch doppelte Ärmeltreffe für Hauptfeldwebel. Hoheitsabzeichen für alle Dienstgrade aus silbergrauem Baumwollgarn auf schwarzer Unterlage, gewebt.

Schwarze Feldhose ohne Vorstöße.

Zur schwarzen Sonderkleidung wird Koppel ohne Seitenwaffe getragen; zu Paraden von Offizieren Feldbinde mit Achselband, von Unteroffizieren und Mannschaften Schützenschnur, soweit verliehen. Schuhwerk: leichte Schnürschuhe.

Another distinguishing feature of the uniform was the use of the death's head on the collar patches. Contrary to modern interpretation, these had no sinister purpose. Instead, it was merely a borrowing from the cavalry tradition, not only of Germany, but also of many other European countries. The death's head on the tanker's uniform continued the traditions of the First World War. The tankers from that conflict had painted a large death's head on the front side of their tanks. The tanker's badge for former tank crews of the First World War that was instituted by the Ministry of Defense on 13 July 1921 also bore a death's head.

At left is the fighting vehicle badge of the Weimar Republic commemorating former crewmembers of armored vehicles of the First World War, featuring the death's head symbol of the *Panzertruppe*.[24]

The musical needs of the force were also addressed with the writing of the "Tanker's Song" by *Leutnant* Wiehle, a young armor officer. It was set to the melody of a hiking song and soon became universally known.[25] It was mandatory to learn the song and it was sung at every ceremonial occasion.

24. Translator's note: There were several varieties of death's heads worn. The one on this badge is the "Brunswick" version. The one worn on the tanker uniform was a different variant.

25. Author's Note: Ritgen, 34.

Panzer-Lied

The *Panzer-Lied* on a prewar postcard.

Panzer-Lied
Whether it's storming or snowing; whether the sun shines upon us;
Whether the day is glowing hot or the night ice cold.
Our faces may be dirty, but we are in high spirits;
Our tank is racing into the storm winds.
With thundering motors, as fast as lightning;
Advancing against the enemy, protected by our tank.
Ahead of our comrades, all by ourselves in the fight;
We advance deeply into the enemy ranks.
If an enemy army then appears in front of us,
We will step on the gas and head into the enemy!
What does our life matter compared to the army of the *Reich*?
To die for Germany is our highest honor.
The enemy holds us up with obstacles and mines;
We laugh at them and go around.
And if guns threaten us up front, hidden in the yellow soil,
We'll look for ways that no one else has found.
And if faithless luck leaves us in the lurch
And we do not return to our homeland,
If a deadly bullet hits us, if fate calls in its hand,
Then our tank is an honorable grave.

5. 1935: Birth of the *Panzertruppe* and *Panzer-Regiment 5*

On 16 March 1935, the government of the *Reich* introduced general conscription, reestablishing the sovereignty of the military. The *Reichswehr* had become the *Wehrmacht*.

Starting in the spring of 1935, the companies of *Kampfwagen-Regiment 1* (Zossen) received 21 tanks (three platoons of seven tanks each). The fourth platoon of each company initially received only dummy vehicles.[26]

In July 1935, during a road march to the Döberitz Training Area, the regiment showed itself in public for the first time. During its stay at the training area, the formation—from individual companies to the regiment—was melded into a cohesive whole by means of exercises.

On the return march to Zossen, a parade was held at the Potsdam gardens by this first element of the new *Panzertruppe* for the Inspector General of Motorized Forces, *Generalleutnant* Lutz.

26. Author's Note: Nehring, 83.

On 25 July 1935, both regiments participated in an exercise at the Zossen Training Area, which was attended not only by the Commander-in-Chief of the Army, *General der Artillerie Freiherr* von Fritsch,[27] but also by Hitler. This was followed by training and testing exercises at the Munster Training Area. While there, Lutz and Guderian proved the value of "combined-arms fighting" through the use of additional fully motorized elements from other branches of service that successfully worked together with the tanks. The effort to create an "armored division" had succeeded thanks to the dynamism, far-sightedness and persistence of its creator, Guderian. The exercises were concluded at the training area with a parade for the Minister of Defense.

From the training area at Munster, the head-quarters of the 2nd Battalion and the 5th Company moved to the Ohrdruf Training Area, where the *ad hoc Panzer-Abteilung Nürnberg* was established under *Major* Breith. In addition to the elements cited

27. Translator Note: *Freiherr* is a term of nobility, indicating a count.

Panzer-Abteilung Nürnberg at the Bückeberg in 1935.

The presentation of the *Panzertruppe* at the *Reich* Party Days in 1935.

above, the battalion was also composed of elements from the rest of *Kampfwagen-Regiment 1* and its sister regiment, *Kampfwagen-Regiment 2*. The mission of the battalion was to present the fledgling *Panzertruppe* to the general public for the first time at the *Reich* Party Days in Nuremberg from 10 to 16 September 1935. The battalion was then paraded at the Bückeberg, which was an annual gathering of farmers, where the armed forces put on displays to demonstrate its importance and capabilities to the agricultural community.

On 27 September 1935, the *Kommando der Kraftfahrkampftruppen* was redesignated as the *Kommando der Panzertruppen*. Lutz, the commanding general, was promoted to become the first *General der Panzertruppen* on 1 November 1935.

On 1 October 1935, *Kampfwagenregiment 2 (Ohrdruf)* was deactivated and the personnel used to form the first four tank regiments: 1, 2, 3 and 4. On 15 October 1935, the first armored contingent of the German Armed Forces, *Kraftfahrlehrkommando Zossen/Kampfwagenregiment 1*, was redesignated as

Panzer-Regiment 5. The command positions of the regiment were occupied as follows on 15 October 1935:[28]

Panzer-Regiment 5

Commander: *Oberstleutnant* Zuckertort

1st Battalion

Commander: *Oberstleutnant* Streich
1st Company: *Hauptmann* Köhn
2nd Company: *Hauptmann* Thomale
3rd Company: *Hauptmann* Linke
4th Company: *Hauptmann* Wendenburg

2nd Battalion

Commander: *Major* Breith
5th Company: *Oberleutnant* von Heinemann
6th Company: *Oberleutnant* Mildebrath
7th Company: *Hauptmann* von Langenthal
8th Company: ?

28. Author's Note: *Geschichte der I. Abteilung des Panzer-Regiments 5*, 1.

Organization of the *3. Panzer-Division* at the End of 1935

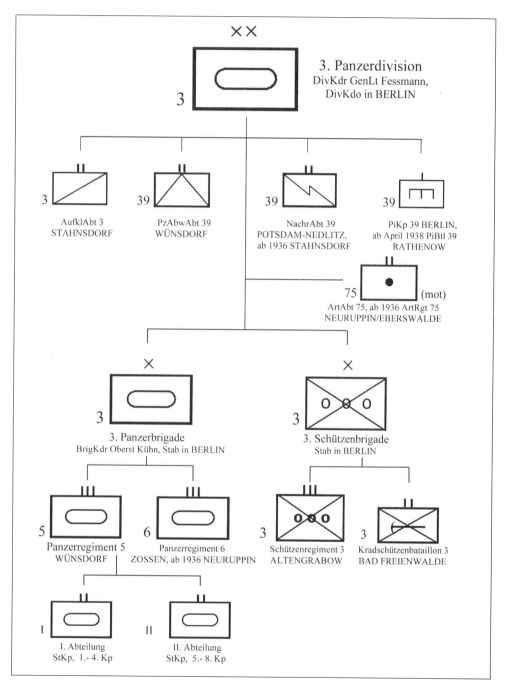

Legend to German entries: *ab* = effective; *DivKdr = Divisionskommandeur* = Division Commander; *Generalleutnant = Generalleutnant*; *DivKdo = Divisions-Kommando* = Division Headquarters; *AufklAbt = Aufklärungs-Abteilung* = Reconnaissance Battalion; *PzAbwAbt = Panzerabwehr-Abteilung* = Antitank Battalion; *NachAbt = Nachrichten-Abteilung* = Signals Battalion; *PiKp = Pionier-Kompanie* = Engineer Company; *ArtAbt = Artillerie-Abteilung* = Artillery Battalion; *ArtRgt = Artillerie-Regiment* = Artillery Regiment; *mot = motorisiert* = motorized; *BrigKdr = Brigade-Kommandeur* = Brigade Commander; *Schützen-Brigade* = Rifle Regiment; *Schützen-Bataillon* = Rifle Battalion; *Kradschützenbataillon* = Motorcycle Infantry Battalion; *Abteilung* = Battalion.

In addition, both of the battalions had a light tank platoon and a signals platoon. The regiment had a maintenance company

15 October 1935 can be considered as the birth date of the *Panzertruppe*. The goal of having a branch of service capable of conducting operational-level missions that stood on its own and with its own command had been realized. Initially, it consisted of three armored divisions, which also had motorized or armored components from other branches of service. The first three armored division that reported to the Armored Forces Command were

1. Panzer-Division (headquartered in Weimar)
Commander: *Generalleutnant* Maximilian *Reichsfreiherr* von Weichs (originally cavalry)
2. Panzer-Division (headquartered in Wurzburg)
Commander: *Oberst* Heinz Guderian (originally infantry, then motorized forces)
3. Panzer-Division (headquartered in Berlin)
Commander: *Generalmajor* Ernst Fessmann (originally cavalry, then motorized forces)

Panzer-Regiment 5 was assigned to the *3. Panzer-Division*. Some claim that the birth date of the regiment was actually 1 October 1934, but since the official designation of *Panzer-Regiment 5* was not used until 15 October 1935, that is the date that will be given precedence in this study.

The establishment of troop elements for the new armored divisions meant that *Panzer-Regiment 5* had to give up considerable amounts of personnel. For instance, the activation of *Panzer-Regiment 6* in Zossen meant that officers and men from *Panzer-Regiment 5* had to be reassigned. In addition, the new regiment received personnel levies from *Reiter-Regiment 4* (Potsdam). Together with *Panzer-Regiment 6*, the two tank regiments formed the *3. Panzer-Brigade* of the *3. Panzer-Division*. In addition to providing personnel for its sister regiment, *Panzer-Regiment 5* also had to provide two complete companies to help establish *Panzer-Regiment 4* on 15 October 1935. The division was organized as follows on 15 October 1935:

The Garrisons of the *3. Panzer-Division* in the Brandenburg Region (see map on next page)
Berlin: Headquarters of both the *3. Panzer-Division* and the *3. Panzer-Brigade*
Eberswalde: Headquarters of the *3. Schützen-Brigade*; *Schützen-Regiment 3*; *II./Artillerie-Regiment 75*
Neuruppin: *Panzer-Regiment 6*; Headquarters and the *I./Artillerie-Regiment 75*
Wünsdorf: *Panzer-Regiment 5*; *Panzerabwehr-Abteilung 39*
Rathenow: *Pionier-Bataillon 39*
Bad Freienwalde: *Kradschützen-Bataillon 3*
Stahnsdorf: *Nachrichten-Abteilung 39*; *Aufklärungs-Abteilung 3*

6. *Panzer-Regiment 5* in the Wünsdorf Garrison

The small town of Wünsdorf, in the province of Teltow, 42 kilometers south of Berlin, was selected as the garrison for *Panzer-Regiment 5*. It had already served as a military garrison during the First World War. The buildings for the infantry gunnery school were constructed there from 1911 to 1913. In 1925, the training battalion of *Infanterie-Regiment 9* (Potsdam) moved there in 1925. It was followed in 1931 by the *3./Preußische Kraftfahr-Abteilung 3*.[29] In 1935, *Panzerabwehr-Abteilung 39* moved in. The garrison was later named the *Hindenburg-Kaserne*.

In addition to the troop units stationed in the garrison, there was also a military gymnastics school. It was established between 1914 and 1916. German athletes trained there for the 1936 Olympics. During the First World War, there were also a number of prisoner-of-war camps erected in the vicinity of Wünsdorf. Also, in 1918, Wünsdorf became the home of the replacement battalion for the German armored forces of the First World War.

The location of various training facilities close by made it a good location for tank training. There was the nearby Zossen Training Area, which had been established in 1907, the Döberitz Training Area, which was approximately 50 kilometers away, and the Kümmersdorf Gunnery Ranges.

In the years 1935–36, there was considerable construction for the new garrisons, on the order of magnitude of some 80 buildings. These were intended for *Panzer-Regiment 5*, the Armor School and the Motorization Training and Testing Battalion. *Panzer-Regiment 5* started moving to Wünsdorf on 20 October 1935. The move was underscored by a large motor march that morning from the previous garrison at Zossen along *Reich* Highway 96 to Wünsdorf. There was a large civilian population present to witness the move, all accompanied by the music of the regimental band.

After the companies moved in, they immediately started work on making the sterile environs more

---

29. Translator's Note: 3rd Company of the 3rd Motorized Battalion (Prussia)

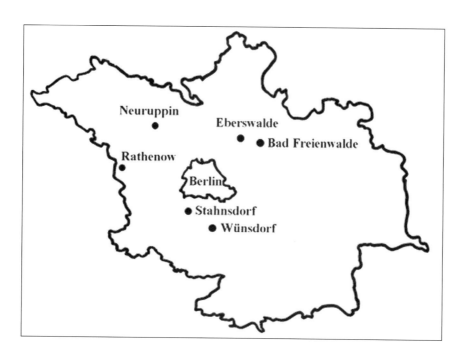

hospitable, so that the soldiers would have a comfortable "home" during their time of service, which would offer comfort and respite after the daily duties. As a result, noncommissioned officer and enlisted common areas were established, as well as reading rooms, table tennis areas and game rooms. All of the rooms had a civilian radio. The windows were decorated with curtains and flower boxes. Commemorative displays were set up in the long hallways.

In addition, gunnery ranges, a small sports facility and a gymnasium were all established using their own means.

The 1st Battalion built a boathouse on Lake Wünsdorf. Members of the battalion had the opportunity to participate in rowing or simply enjoy the water there. Many recruits from all areas of Germany thus became acquainted with the beautiful local scenery.

In October 1935, the regiment received its first conscripts from the reintroduction of the draft in March of that year.[30] The were sworn in along with the other recruits of the garrison in a ceremony on 7 November.

30. Author's Note: *Geschichte der I. Abteilung des Panzer-Regiments 5*, 1.

Map from 1940 of Wünsdorf and Its Garrisons

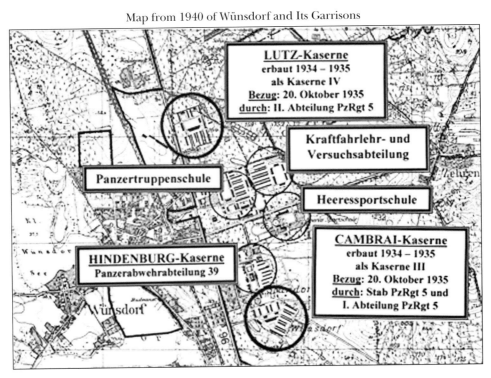

Legend: *Lutz-Kaserne*: Built 1934–35 as Garrison IV. Occupied on 20 October 1935 by the *II./Panzer-Regiment 5*.

Panzertruppenschule: Armor School.

Kraftfahrlehr- und . . . : Motorization Training and Testing Battalion.

Heeressportschule: Army Sports School.

Hindenburg-Kaserne: *Panzerabwehr-Abteilung 39*.

Cambrai-Kaserne: Built 1934–35 as Garrison III. Occupied on 20 October 1935 by the Headquarters of *Panzer-Regiment 5* and the *I./Panzer-Regiment 5*.

20 October 1935: The commander of *Panzer-Regiment 5*, *Oberstleutnant* Zuckertort, enters the garrison of Wünsdorf, signified by the white tape, as the first vehicle after moving along *Reich* Highway 96. His vehicle is the command version of the *Panzer I*, the *Panzerbefehlswagen I*.

20 October 1935: The 1st Battalion of *Panzer-Regiment 5* enters Garrison III with its vehicles. The garrison was christened the *Cambrai-Kaserne* on 22 February 1938. To the left is the battalion headquarters; to the right is the regimental headquarters.

20 October 1935: *Oberstleutnant* Zuckertort after arriving at the new garrison.

The 2nd Battalion was billeted in Garrison IV, which was later christened the *General-Lutz-Kaserne*. View from the garrison in the direction of *Reich* Highway 96. To the left is the battalion headquarters; on the right is the billet of the 5th Company.

A postcard of *General-Lutz-Kaserne* in 1936. The Fighting Vehicle Memorial, which was dedicated on 16 March 1936, featured a "heavy tractor" from the KAMA Armor School. The billets of the 5th Company are on the left, one of the battalion mess halls is in the middle and the billet of the 6th Company is on the right.

The boathouse of the 1st Battalion of the regiment along Lake Wünsdorf.

Bronze memorial of the 2nd Battalion of *Panzer-Regiment 5* in Wünsdorf. It reads: "In the Spirit of Comrades from the World War: Attack—Fight—Win." Both this memorial and the one below feature the only German tank of the First World War, the *A7V*.

Overview of the Process of Establishing *Panzer-Regiment 5*

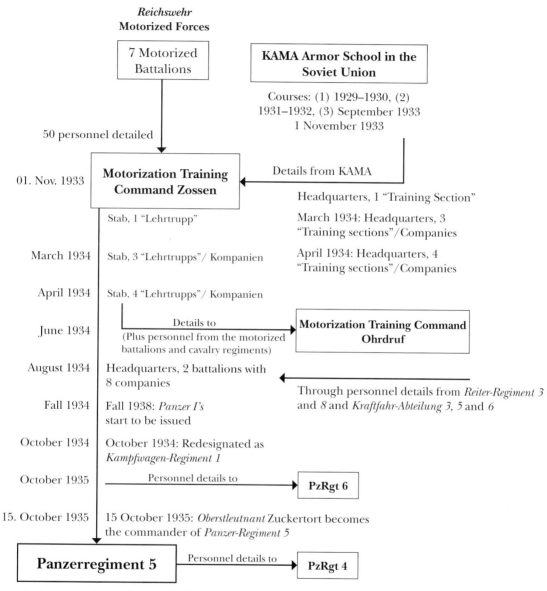

Reichswehr
Motorized Forces

7 Motorized
Battalions

**KAMA Armor School in the
Soviet Union**

Courses: (1) 1929–1930, (2)
1931–1932, (3) September 1933
1 November 1933

50 personnel detailed

01. Nov. 1933   **Motorization Training
Command Zossen**   Details from KAMA

Headquarters, 1 "Training Section"

Stab, 1 "Lehrtrupp"

March 1934   Stab, 3 "Lehrtrupps"/ Kompanien   March 1934: Headquarters, 3
"Training sections"/Companies

April 1934   Stab, 4 "Lehrtrupps"/ Kompanien   April 1934: Headquarters, 4
"Training sections"/Companies

June 1934   Details to   **Motorization Training Command
Ohrdruf**
(Plus personnel from the motorized
battalions and cavalry regiments)

August 1934   Headquarters, 2 battalions with
8 companies

Through personnel details from *Reiter-Regiment 3*
and *8* and *Kraftfahr-Abteilung 3, 5* and *6*

Fall 1934   Fall 1938: *Panzer I's*
start to be issued

October 1934   October 1934: Redesignated as
Kampfwagen-Regiment 1

October 1935   Personnel details to   **PzRgt 6**

15. October 1935   15 October 1935: *Oberstleutnant* Zuckertort becomes
the commander of *Panzer-Regiment 5*

Panzerregiment 5   Personnel details to   **PzRgt 4**

Headquarters; 2 battalions with 8 line
companies; maintenance company

Adolf Hitler visits Zossen before the war.

Krupp-Daimler *Sd.Kfz. 3* of *Kraftfahr-Abteilung 4*. Like all of the other motorized battalions of the *Reichswehr*, it had to provide personnel for the establishment of the Motorization Training Command Zossen. The soldier in the middle is the future *Hauptmann* Bassenge, who was a member of the regiment from 1937 to 1939, ending his assignment there as the company commander of the 3rd Company.

One of the first: Kurt Helms, born on 19 July 1912 in Schönebeck on the Elbe. At 17, he entered the military. In November 1933, he was transferred from *Kraftfahr-Abteilung 4* to Motorization Training Command Zossen. In the image, he is wearing the uniform of a member of the motorized battalion. Upon his transfer, he started training new recruits in the 1st Company in April 1934 as a noncommissioned officer. After the training command was redesignated as *Panzer-Regiment 5*, he was transferred to the regimental headquarters and later became the First Sergeant of the 5th Company. He participated in the campaigns in Poland, France and North Africa. In 1942, he was captured at El Alamein.

23 April 1934: Swearing-in ceremony for recruits at Zossen. All the way to the left is *Hauptmann* Conze, the commander of the 1st Company. The 2nd Company can be seen in the far right of the image.

Transitional training from horses and trucks to tankers. In November 1934, the black tanker uniform was introduced, which initially featured no national insignia. They were not added until the beginning of November 1935.

A Model A *Panzer I* at the Zossen Training Area. Until 1940, the *Panzer I* was the mainstay of the tank regiments. It had originally been conceived as solely a training and exercise vehicle. Operations in Spain, Poland, France and North Africa quickly demonstrated that neither its armor nor armament were capable of standing up to a fight against enemy armor. By the end of 1941, it had disappeared from front-line service, except in a variety of special-purpose modifications.

Zossen, 1934: Soldiers of the training command after a combat exercise.

1934: An evening social. An apple wine cooler cost 15 *Pfennig*.

Spring of 1935: Combat training on a *Panzer I*.

11 May 1935: Cleaning and maintenance of personal clothing and equipment.

Potsdam, July 1935: the first public parade of the Motorization Training Command Zossen.

August 1935: Instructional and testing exercises. Divisional-level exercise involving combined arms at the Munster Training Area. In the middle of the picture is *Oberstleutnant i.G.* Walther K. Nehring, who was the operations officer of the Inspectorate for Motorized Combat Forces in the Ministry of Defense. He was a close associate of Heinz Guderian, the "Creator of the *Panzertruppe.*" (Photo courtesy of the Chr. Nehring)

Postcard view of exercises with *Panzer I's* at a training area.

14–17 September 1935: *Panzer-Abteilung Nürnberg* at the *Reich* Party Days at Nuremberg. The *ad hoc* battalion was composed of elements of both the Zossen and Ohrdruf motorization training commands under the command of *Major* Breith, who is seen here in the lead *Panzer I*. He was the commander of the Zossen command's 2nd Battalion, effective 1 August 1934.

18 June 1935: The Motorization Training Command Zossen had its own band.

20 October 1935: *Oberstleutnant* Zuckertort, the commander of *Panzer-Regiment 5*, enters the grounds of the Wünsdorf garrison after road-marching on *Reich* Highway 96 from Zossen. His command and control vehicle, a *Panzerbefehlswagen I*, breaks the white tape that had been placed across the road.

The *Cambrai-Kaserne* in Wünsdorf. It was initially built under contract from the Army Construction Office in Berlin from 1934 to 1935 as Garrison III. It was occupied on 20 October 1935 by the headquarters of *Panzer-Regiment 5* and its 1st Battalion (Commander: *Major* Streich).

Guard force in front of the *Cambrai-Kaserne* (period postcard). A soldier of the regiment sounded the trumpet three times daily: "Reveille" (0600 hours), "Prelude to Taps" (2045 hours) and "Taps" (2100 hours).

Another view of the armor memorial at the *Cambrai-Kaserne* (period postcard).

A close-up view of the *A7V* modeled in the memorial.

General-Lutz-Kaserne along *Reich* Highway 96 in Wünsdorf-Zossen. It was built under contract from the Army Construction Office in Berlin from 1934 to 1935 as Garrison IV. It was occupied on 20 October 1935 by the 2nd Battalion of *Panzer-Regiment 5* (Commander: *Major* Breith).

Marker on the company billets of the 7th Company in Wünsdorf.

Memorial in front of the company. The First Sergeant of the company, *Oberfeldwebel* Rother, can be seen on the left. To his left is *Oberleutnant* Lossen.

Conscription was reintroduced in Germany on 16 March 1935. The first draftees for *Panzer-Regiment 5* are greeted at the Wünsdorf train station and escorted back to the garrison by the regimental band.

October 1935: Draftees for the 1st Battalion of *Panzer-Regiment 5* enter the garrison.

7 November 1935: Swearing in recruits at the *General-Lutz-Kaserne*.

The regimental band. The soldiers were assigned to the headquarters of the regiment.

The bandmaster was *Musikmeister* Taeger.

CHAPTER 2

Panzer-Regiment 5
from 1936 to August 1939

1. 1936

During the early-morning hours of 25 February 1936, the troop elements of the *3. Panzer-Division*, including *Panzer-Regiment 5*, were alerted. Ammunition was issued and loaded up. In anticipation of the intended German occupation of the Rhineland, which had been declared a demilitarized zone by the Treaty of Versailles, the division was sent to Camp Senne Training Area by rail.

The Armored Forces Command conducted exercises there with its armored and motorized forces, in the event it proved unnecessary to provide countermeasures to a military intervention on the part of the Western Powers. The forces were not employed and returned to their garrisons later that month.

✠

On 16 March, the commander of the 2nd Battalion, *Oberstleutnant* Breith, dedicated the "Fighting Vehicle Memorial" near the entrance to the *General-Lutz-Kaserne*. The centerpiece of the memorial was a 20-ton experimental combat vehicle ("heavy tractor") from 1928, which was mounted on large boulders. According to Breith: "It is intended as a symbol of our unshakeable martial spirit and as an incentive to the work in forming the battalion."

The Fighting Vehicle Memorial in *General-Lutz-Kaserne* in front of the headquarters building of the 2nd Battalion across from the entrance to the post. The photograph was taken from a window in the billet of the 6th Company.

On 20 April, the first large-scale parade of the Armed Forces was held on the occasion of the birthday of the head of state. The regiment participated in the parade.

The 2nd Battalion sponsored a "Tank Sports Fest" at the Zossen Training Area on 28 June. Under wonderful summer skies, some 30,000 visitors from the immediate vicinity and also Berlin watched the events.[1] Some of the events: synchronized gymnastics with 200 men; acrobatics on moving motorcycles;

1. Author's Note: *Geschichte der II./Panzer-Regiment 5,*

negotiation of large obstacles by tanks; chariot racing; remotely controlled motorcycles; and trapeze artists. Thanks to the photographs placed on display, one could trace the development of fighting vehicles from the scythe chariots of ancient times through the assault carts of the Middle Ages to the tanks of the Great War. The high point of the day was a combat exercise put on by the entire 2nd Battalion.

Of course, 1936 was also marked by several visits to training areas by the two battalions of the regiment. Company-, battalion- and regiment-level

Panzer I's of the 2nd Battalion crash through obstacles.

Program for the "Tank Sport Fest" held at the Zossen Training Area on 28 June.

training was conducted at Döberitz from 28 May to 9 June and again from 20 August to 9 September. Gunnery training was conducted at Putlos from 29 July to 9 August.

On 26 September, the first recruits to the battalion were released from active duty by the regimental commander after a field service and farewell address.

In October, the regiment had to release soldiers for the activation of a new formation. The Signals Platoon of the 1st Battalion and the 3rd and 6th Companies were sent to Zossen to form *Panzer-Regiment 8.* In addition, a few officers were also reassigned.

The tanks were equipped with short-wave radios and intercom sets in 1936. It was only through voice radio that the leaders could affect the forces in the fight by means of their own voice and their personal temperament. Up to that point, signal flags had been used.

Panzer I's of the 2nd Battalion at a training area.

The 1st Battalion has formed up in the *Cambrai-Kaserne* to perform vehicle maintenance. The water tower between the *Cambrai Kaserne* and the *Hindenburg-Kaserne* can be seen in the background.

Training on the *Panzer Ia* in the area of the maintenance bays of the regiment in Wünsdorf.

The soldiers of the regiment received multifaceted and thorough training in the garrisons at Wünsdorf.

The Army High Command directed the formation of troop elements in September, which were to be sent to Spain to help the royalist forces of Franco in their fight against the Republican Spaniards who were supported by the Soviet Union. A first contingent, consisting of 32 *Panzer I's*, was already on its way to Spain in October.[2] The vehicles and personnel came from *Panzer-Regiment 4* and *Panzer-Regiment 6*. Soldiers from *Panzer-Regiment 5* also volunteered. They were discharged from the

army so that they could fight for a foreign army in a different uniform. Contrary to the airmen of the *Luftwaffe*,[3] the soldiers of the *Panzertruppe* primarily provided support and training.

Starting on 30 October, the *Panzer I's* with Spanish crews were used less for pure armor missions; instead, they were more frequently used to reinforce the infantry. Operational experience with the machine-gun-equipped tanks confirmed the demands of the forces in the field for armored vehicles equipped with larger caliber main guns and heavier armor.

2. Author's Note: Jentz, *Die deutsche Panzertruppe*, Vol. 1, 45.

3. The *Luftwaffe* units, organized as the volunteer "*Condor Legion*," participated directly in combat operations.

Panzer I's in service during the Spanish Civil War (1936–1939).

View from the headquarters building of the 2nd Battalion of the regiment of the memorial dedicated on 16 March in the *General-Lutz-Kaserne.* To the left are the billets of the 6th, 7th and 8th Companies.

The memorial consisted of a 20-ton "Experimental Combat Vehicle" (*Großtraktor*) dating from 1928.

A pass-in-review is conducted in front of the commander and his staff after a swearing-in ceremony for recruits. To the right is the regimental band.

Spring 1936: The day room for the noncommissioned officers of the 7th Company is "broken in." To the right is the company commander, *Oberleutnant* von Heinemann (15 October 1935–15 October 1936). In the middle of the picture is the commander of the 2nd Battalion, *Oberstleutnant* Hermann Breith. Breith went on to receive the Knight's Cross to the Iron Cross on 3 June 1940 as an *Oberst* and the commander of the *5. Panzer-Brigade.* The Oak Leaves to the Knight's Cross followed on 31 January 1942 as a *Generalmajor* and commander of the *3. Panzer-Division* (69th recipient of the award). On 21 February 1944, he became the 48th member of the German Armed Forces to be honored with the Swords to the Oak Leaves to the Knight's Cross as a *General der Panzertruppen* and the commanding general of the *III. Panzer-Korps.* Next to Breith is the First Sergeant of the company, *Oberfeldwebel* Rother.

Another photograph from the same gathering.

Leutnant Braun's room. Braun was assigned to the
7th Company.

Hijinks in the barracks.

Berlin. Parade der Wehrmacht.
Tanks am Brandenburger Tor

April 1936: Parade in honor of Hitler's birthday. *Panzer I's* of the 2nd Battalion of the regiment at the *Brandenburger Tor* (period postcard). The tanks are painted in the prewar three-tone camouflage pattern of green, brown and dark yellow. The battalion and regimental numerals can clearly be seen flanking the tactical symbol for armor, the rhomboid.

1936 was marked by a number of tactical exercises for the regiment, as well as gunnery training. This photograph shows a company's tanks being set up for inspection by the battalion commander.

Panzer I moving cross-country.

9 June 1936: Rations are issued for the 1st Battalion of the regiment on the move back from the Döberitz Training Area.

5 July 1936: The regimental band and a choir from the 7th Company during a performance on the Berlin radio station.

Personal clothing and equipment inspection in the *Cambrai-Kaserne.*

End of 1936: A *Panzer I* of the 2nd Battalion during an exercise. Note the use of signal flags.

Another view of the *Panzer Ia* seen above. The earliest model of the *Panzer I* was most easily identified by having only four roadwheels and three return rollers. The idler wheel served as a quasi fifth roadwheel. Later models of the vehicles had five roadwheels, four return rollers and an elevated idler arm.

2. 1937

Another training year started. New recruits arrived and were sworn in in a large ceremony for all of the garrisons based in Wünsdorf.

A special event occurred on the evening of 19 April 1937. On the *Wilhelmsplatz* in Berlin, Hitler presented 90 standards or flags to new formations of the three major branches of the German Armed Forces. The motorized formations received standards, and both battalions of the regiment were presented theirs from the hand of Hitler.[4]

The year 1937 was also marked by numerous rotations to training areas, such Groß Born in

---

4. Author's Note: *Geschichte der I./Panzer-Regiment 5*, 2, and *Geschichte der II./Panzer-Regiment 5*, 4.

1937: Swearing in recruits for the Wünsdorf garrisons at the *General-Lutz-Kaserne*. The ceremony was concluded with a pass-in-review.

Troop standards for mounted, horse-drawn and motorized battalions of the armed forces. The basic color of the standard was the branch-of-service color. In this case, the rose pink of the *Panzertruppe*.

As in the previous year, the battalions of the regiment participated in the armed forces birthday parade for the *Führer*. The newly awarded standards were carried in the vehicles past the Commander-in-Chief.

Pomerania (June), followed by gunnery training at Putlos on the Baltic.

In June 1937, veterans of Germany's World War I tank arm met at Wünsdorf, founding a veteran's association.[5] The lineage and honors of the old tank arm, previously maintained by the regiment, were transferred to the Armor School. In addition, there were historical associations maintained with the "old army." The 1st Battalion maintained the traditions of the Guards Cuirassiers; the 2nd Battalion the 2nd Guards Ulan Regiment. The *Revue-Marsch* was selected as the regimental march.

From 21 August to 16 September, the regiment was at the Bergen Training Area to prepare for the

fall maneuvers that were to follow. Exercises were conducted within the framework of the *3. Panzer-Brigade* and the *3. Panzer-Division*. The highlight of the training year was the participation in the Armed Forces Maneuvers from 19 to 29 September in Mecklenburg, which was also referred to as the "Mussolini Maneuvers" by the tankers in the regiment. On 26 September, an attack by the *1. Panzer-Brigade* and the *3. Panzer-Brigade* under the command of *Generalleutnant* Guderian was demonstrated in the presence of both Hitler and Mussolini.

In the summer of 1937, the *Panzer II* began to be issued. It was intended to complement the *Panzer I*. The two tanks met the military requirement of the time to initially provide the *Panzertruppe* with numerous light tanks.

---

5. Author's Note: *Traditionsvereinigung ehemaliger Angehöriger der Panzertruppe des Weltkriegs*. Translator's Note: Association of Former Members of the Armored Forces of the World War.

"In the heat of battle": A *Panzer Ib* (top) backed into a *Panzer 1a* during an exercise.

Panzerkampfwagen II

(*Sd.Kfz. 121*)

Model C

Technical Data for the C Model

Length:	4.81 meters
Width:	2.28 meters
Height:	2.02 meters
Combat weight:	8.9 tons
Horsepower:	140
Maximum speed (road):	40 kilometers an hour
Range (road):	150 kilometers
Fuel capacity:	170 liters
Crew:	3
Armament:	2-centimter Model 38 Automatic Cannon; 1 7.92-millimeter Model 34 machine gun
Basic load of main-gun ammunition:	180
Armor:	
Front slope:	3 centimeters
Driver's compartment:	3 centimeters
Sides:	1.5 centimeters
Rear:	1.4 centimeters
Turret front:	3 centimeters
Price (minus weapons):	49,228 *Reichsmark*

1. Author's Note: Quarrie, *Das große Buch der Deutschen Heeres,* 188.
2. Author's Note: Data sheets for Army Weapons, vehicles and Equipment, Sheet G 300, 136.

In October, the regiment provided its 5th and 6th Companies, as well as a number of officers, to help form *Panzer-Regiment 15* in Sagan. In addition, the commander of the 1st Battalion, *Oberstleutnant* Streich, was also reassigned there. Half of the 8th Company was reassigned to the Gunnery School at Putlos.

On 13 October, *Oberst i.G.* Nehring, a close associate of Guderian, assumed command of the re-

giment from *Oberst* Zuckertort. Nehring, who would go on to become a highly decorated and successful armor general, brought ideal prerequisites with him for the job. Together with Guderian, he had created the doctrinal principles for the employment of modern armored forces and, consequently, must be considered one of the founders of the armored force. As a regimental commander, he was about to transform theory into practice.

Nehring was a hard taskmaster and demanded much, but he also understood how to convey that what was demanded had a purpose and was necessary.[6] About the same time, there was also a change in division command. The new commander effective 1 October was *Generalleutnant Freiherr* Geyr von Schweppenburg.

6. Author's Note: Paul, *Panzer-General Walther K. Nehring*, 73.

Assumption of command by *Oberst i.G.* Nehring on 13 October in Wünsdorf.

January 1937: Small-arms training at the garrison ranges.

Tank gunnery training for the 6th Company.

Hauptmann Theodor Schimmelmann *Graf* von Lindenburg, company commander of the 6th from 15 October 1936 to 15 October 1937. He received the Knight's Cross to the Iron Cross on 14 May 1941 as a *Major* and commander of the *II./Panzer-Regiment 15*. In addition, he was also awarded the German Cross in Gold (3 February 1943).

Another view of the tank gunnery training for the 6th Company.

A view from a neighboring tank.

A *Panzer Ia* of the 1st Battalion.

Maintenance is performed on the tanks in front of the tank bays at *Cambrai-Kaserne.*

From June to August, *Leutnant* Braun of the 6th Company conducted noncommissioned officer course for the 2nd Battalion. In this photograph, training is being conducted on the Bergmann MP 28/II submachine gun. In the background are the billets of the 5th Company.

Drill and ceremonies are practiced on the parade grounds at the *General-Lutz-Kaserne*. In the left background is the billets for the Headquarters Company. To the right is the 5th Company.

The soldier is explaining the misses.

Marksmanship training. The instructor is attempting to determine whether the recruit is taking up a good sight picture. The noncommissioned officer can be identified as a member of a 5th Regiment because of the chain-stitched numeral on his should straps. In this case, it is for *Panzer-Regiment 5.*

Tanker recruits were not spared the bane of harassment, either. In this case, "hitting the deck and recovering" on the parade grounds.

Training on the Model 08 pistol, the famous Luger.

Returning from infantry training.

Recruits pose with their drill sergeants and an officer in front of the Fighting Vehicle Memorial and the headquarters building of the 2nd Battalion in the *General-Lutz-Kaserne*.

Tanks of the 1st Company at a training
area. Note the wearing of neckties, even
with the field uniform, a practice that
often continued even under wartime
conditions.

Starting in the summer,
the regiment started to be
issued the *Panzer II*. This
is an *Ausf. A*. The *Panzer II*
was armed with a 2.0-cm
rapid firing cannon.

Training demonstration: The *Panzer II* crosses a water obstacle. The prewar three-color (green, brown and yellow) camouflage has been applied to this vehicle and portions of it can easily be seen on the turret.

The regiment was at the Bergen Training Area from 21 August to 16 September in preparation for the fall maneuvers. The command and control variant of the *Panzer I* can be seen on the left.

An early *Panzer I* in the background and an early *Panzer II* in the foreground.

A *Panzerbefehlswagen* leads a column of tanks.

Above: A *Panzer II* of the 2nd Company, to which field camouflage—cut vegetation—has been applied. Below: A *Panzer II* in a concealed position.

The exercise is over. As was customary in the German Army, a few songs were sung.

The commander of the 1st Battalion, *Oberstleutnant* Johannes Streich, takes his luncheon meal.

The battalion commander and his company commanders. *Oberstleutnant* Johannes Streich is to the viewer's left rear. He was the commander from 15 October 1936 to 15 October 1937, when he was transferred to Sagan to take command of the newly forming *Panzer-Regiment 15* (initially *5. Panzer-Division*; later *11. Panzer-Division*). In February 1941, as a *Generalmajor*, he became the commander of the *5. leichte Division* in Africa. Next to him is *Hauptmann* Gierga, the commander of the 1st Company; *Major* Seupel, the 3rd Company; and *Hauptmann* von Wilcke, the 2nd Company. As a *Major*, von Wilcke later became the commander of the 2nd Battalion on 10 November 1938. Sitting (from the viewer's left): *Hauptmann* Gerhard Wendenburg, the commander of the 4th. He later received the Knight's Cross to the Iron Cross on 15 August 1940 as a *Major* and the commander of *Panzer-Abteilung 67* in the *8. Panzer-Division*. Finally: *Leutnant* Reidel, the battalion adjutant.

The vehicles assemble after the exercise to perform post-operations maintenance.

A *Panzer I* passes a regimental band.

On the return to the garrison in Wünsdorf. Here: *Panzerschütze* Josef Wegener of the 2nd Company in the turret of a *Panzer I*. The camouflage scheme is easy to see in this photograph.

Oberst Nehring (viewer's right), with his son Christopher, after the assumption of command on 13 October. He is conversing with the commander of the 2nd Battalion, *Oberstleutnant* Breith. (Photograph courtesy of Christopher Nehring)

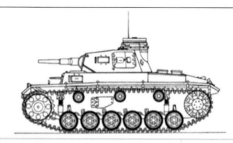

	Panzerkampfwagen III (*Sd.Kfz. 141*) Model E
Characteristics:	6 roadwheels with torsion bars; 3 return rollers; initially, a 3.7-centimeter main gun, followed by a 5-centimeter and, ultimately, a long-barreled 5-centimeter main gun

Technical Data for the Model E	
Length:	5.38 meters
Width:	2.91 meters
Height:	2.44 meters
Combat Weight:	19.5 tons
Horsepower:	300
Maximum speed (road):	40 kilometers an hour
Operating radius (road):	165 kilometers
Fuel capacity:	320 liters
Crew:	5
Armament:	3.7-centimeter, L45 main gun; 2 7.92-millimeter Model 34 machine guns
Basic load of main-gun ammunition:	120 rounds
Armor:	
Front slope, driver's compartment:	3 centimeters
Sides, rear:	2 centimeters
Turret front:	3 centimeters
In the course of the war, additional armor was bolted on to the front slope and gun mantlet of the turret, resulting in up to 8 centimeters of protection on the Models G, H and J, with a corresponding increase in over-all weight to 25 tons and a decrease in over-all performance	
Price (minus weapons):	96,163 *Reichsmark*

1. Author's Note: Spielberger and Wiener, *Die deutschen Panzerkampfwagen III und IV*, 90–91.
2. Author's note: Vehicle data sheets, Sheet G 305, 140.

3. 1938

The next year, 1938, was an event-filled one for the regiment and saw the introduction of both the *Panzer III* and the *Panzer IV*.[7]

Initially, the *Panzer IV* was only intended to be a support vehicle for the lights tank, the *Panzer I's* and *II's*, which made up most of the fleet. The short barrel—24 calibers—did not have enough penetrative capability to directly engage enemy tanks. The robust and reliable design allowed for continual modification, eventually resulting in models with long-barreled 7.5-centimeter main guns—a gun with 48 calibers of length starting in 1942—that were used until the end of the war. The *Panzer IV* ultimately became the standard German main battle tank for all tank regiments.

7. Author's Note: Kampe, *Wünsdorf*, 36.

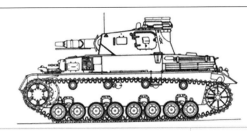

	Panzerkampfwagen IV (*Sd.Kfz. 161*) Model D
Characteristics:	8 roadwheels arranged in pairs on leaf-spring suspension arms; 4 return rollers; initially, a 24-caliber 7.5-centimeter main gun, followed in 1942 by a long-barreled 7.5-centimeter main gun

Technical Data for the Model D

Length:	5.91 meters
Width:	2.86 meters
Height:	2.68 meters
Combat Weight:	20 tons
Horsepower:	300
Maximum speed (road):	40 kilometers an hour
Operating radius (road):	200 kilometers
Fuel capacity:	470 liters
Crew:	5
Armament:	7.5-centimeter, L24 main gun; 2 7.92-millimeter Model 34 machine guns
Basic load of main-gun ammunition:	80 rounds

Armor:

Front slope, driver's compartment, sides and rear:	3 centimeters
Turret front:	3 centimeters

In the course of the war, additional armor was bolted on to the front slope and front areas of the turret, resulting in up to 8.0 centimeters of protection on the Models H and J

Price (minus weapons):	96,163 *Reichsmark*

In all, 8,500 *Panzer IV's* were produced.

1. Author's Note: von Senger und Etterlin, 302–3.
2. Author's note: Vehicle data sheets, Sheet G 315, 143.

February 1938, Wünsdorf: *General der Panzertruppen* Lutz takes his leave of the force he helped create.

March 1938: Officer corps of the 2nd Battalion of the regiment.

On 4 February 1938, the first commanding general of the *Panzertruppe*, Oswald Lutz, retired. He was replaced by *Generalleutnant* Guderian.

As in the previous two years, the regiment took part in the *Führer* Parade in Berlin on 20 April.

Starting on 22 June, general inspections of the companies were held, attended, in part, by the new senior officer of the *Panzertruppe*, *Generalleutnant* Guderian.

A gunnery rotation at the Baumholder Training Area was followed by tactical exercises at the Bergen Training Area in August. Training was conducted at the battalion and regimental level and emphasized combined-arms operations with infantry, antitank forces, combat engineers, artillery and the *Luftwaffe*. Nehring and his regiment were at the center of the exercises. At the time, the 1st Battalion was commanded by *Major* Schaefer, the 2nd by *Major* von Wilcke. Part of the rotation also included a gunnery competition from moving vehicles, which was won by *Hauptmann* Wendenburg's 5th Company.[8] The

8. Author's Note: *Geschichte der 3. Panzer-Division*, 8.

Panzer I's and *Panzer II's* negotiate water obstacles. In the one image, the chassis of an early-model *Panzer I* can be seen forming the support for the expedient bridge.

training rotations were closed out that year with a visit to the Königsbrück Training Area.

During the night of 23–24 September, the regiment was alerted, along with the rest of the division, and loaded on trains at Wünsdorf and Zossen for transport to Ratibor in Upper Silesia. The German Armed Forces occupied the *Sudetenland* as part of the agreement reached in the Munich Accords among Germany, France, Great Britain and Italy.

From 8 to 10 October, the regiment marched across the German frontier into the Troppau area, enthusiastically greeted by the German-speaking local populace.

The lead elements of the regiment cross the border in the direction of Troppau.

The ethnic Germans of the *Sudetenland* had suffered greatly in the face of Czech oppression and longed for a unification with Germany. The banner says: The *Sudetenland* greets the German Armed Forces.

Entry of German forces into Waltersdorf on 9 October.

On 22 October, the regiment returned to Wünsdorf by road marching on the Breslau-Berlin *Autobahn*. A few days later, as in the previous years, personnel levies were placed on the regiment to help form other elements as part of the expansion of the army. The continued reassignments caused a great deal of unrest among the soldiers. The 3rd Company and numerous personnel from the 2nd Battalion were reassigned to Schweinfurt as cadre for *Panzer-Regiment 36* of the newly forming *4. Panzer-Division.* The former commander of the 2nd Battalion, *Oberstleutnant* Breith, was named as the commander of *Panzer-Regiment 36.* Efforts were immediately undertaken in Wünsdorf to form a "new" 2nd Battalion.[9]

On 20 November, after being promoted to *General der Panzertruppen,* Guderian was designated as the "Head of Fast Forces." This consolidation of the so-called "fast forces"—armor, antitank, armored reconnaissance, motorized riles and cavalry—corresponded to a request that had been made by Hitler.[10]

---

9. Author's Note: Kampe, 37.

10. Author's Note: Nehring, 101. According to Nehring (page 113), the term *schnelle Truppen* was replaced by *Panzertruppe* on 1 April 1943.

A pass-in-review is conducted after a swearing-in ceremony in the *General-Lutz-Kaserne.* To the right rear, a *Panzer IV* of the 4th Company can be seen.

6th Company *Panzer-Regiment 5*: Wünsdorf Training Schedule for 25 November 1938

Time:	Activity:	Location:	Responsibility:
0545	First Call		Charge of Quarters
0645	Formation	Company Area	
	Recruits		
0700–0800	NCO Instruction on the *P08*	Rooms	Section leaders
0815–0930	Basic training (drill & ceremonies): Base position; direction; saluting; turning movements	Parade ground	*Leutnant* Kuhn & *Leutnant* Köppen
0945	Marksmanship training with the *P08*	Parade ground	*Leutnant* Kuhn
1130	Receipt of rations	Mess hall	Charge of Quarters
1330	Movement to the gymnasium (Garrison Chaplain Bielecke speaking)		
1500–1630	Training on the *Panzer I* (repeat)	Motor Pool Bays	*Feldwebel* Hosfeld
1645–1745	Officer instruction: Importance of the oath and service obligations	Lecture Hall	*Leutnant* Kuhn
1800	Issuance of orders		*Feldwebel* Klink
	Remainder of the Company		
0700–1100	Maintenance	Motor Pool Bays	*Unteroffizier* Steen
1330–1730	Maintenance	Motor Pool Bays	*Unteroffizier* Steen
	Radio Operators		
1700–1750	Morse Code training	Lecture Hall	*Unteroffizier* Simon
	Post Staff Duty Officer:	*Leutnant* Ilking (Antitank Battalion)	
	Battalion Staff Duty Officer:	*Feldwebel* Gröger (8th Company)	
	Charge of Quarters:	*Unteroffizier* Ott	
	Assistant Charge of Quarters:	*Panzeroberschütze* Schulz	
	Challenge:	*Eberswalde*	
		/signed/ Peter	
		Hauptmann and Company Commander	

Training Schedule for the 6th Company for 30 November 1938

6th Company *Panzer-Regiment 5* Wünsdorf		Training Schedule for 30 November 1938
	Post Staff Duty Officer:	*Leutnant* Hennig (Heavy Company)
	Battalion Staff Duty Officer:	*Feldwebel* Flemming (7th Company)

	Charge of Quarters:	*Unteroffizier* Wildförster	
	Assistant Charge of Quarters:	*Panzeroberschütze* Struth	
	Challenge:	*Grimm*	
Time:	**Activity:**	**Location:**	**Responsibility:**
0545	First Call		Charge of Quarters;
0645	Formation	Company Area	*Feldwebel* Klink
	Recruits		
	1st Platoon		
0700–0800	Officer Instruction on gunnery terminology: Trajectory terms	Lecture Hall	*Leutnant* Kuhn
0815–0945	Basic training (drill & ceremonies): Base position; stationary turning movements; turning movements on the move	Parade ground	*Leutnant* Kuhn
1000–1100	Marksmanship training with the *P08*	Parade ground	*Leutnant* Kuhn
	2nd Platoon, 1st Section		
0700–1100	Driver's training in accordance with schedule	"Shifting" meadows	*Feldwebel* Helpup
	2nd Section		
0700–0845	Hands-on maintenance training on the *Panzer I*	Moto Pool Bays	*Leutnant* Köppen
0900–1100	Maintenance training: Transfer of power and the engine	Lecture Hall	*Leutnant* Köppen
1130	Receipt of rations	Mess hall	Charge of Quarters
	1st Platoon		
1330–1430	NCO Training: *P08*	Rooms	Section leaders; *Feldwebel* Helpup
1445–1630	Basic training on the *Panzer I*: Mounting and dismounting; Opening hatches and buttoning up; Installing and dismounting the weapons	Motor Pool Bays	*Leutnant* Kuhn
1645–1730	Weapons cleaning	Lecture Hall	*Leutnant* Köppen
	2nd Platoon, 1st Group		
1330–1730	Driver's training in accordance with schedule	"Shifting" meadows	*Feldwebel* Helpup
	2nd Group		
1330–1445	Instruction on the *Panzer I*	Motor Pool Bays	*Leutnant* Köppen
1500–1730	Maintenance training: Transfer of power and the engine	Lecture Hall	*Leutnant* Köppen
	Radio Operators		
1700–1750	Morse Code training	Lecture Hall	*Unteroffizier* Simon
		/signed/ Peter	
		Hauptmann and Company Commander	

Hauptmann Ritter Edler von Peter, the company commander of the 6th Company from 1938 to 1939. He received the Knight's Cross to the Iron Cross on 15 July 1941 as a *Major* and the commander of the 1st Battalion of *Panzer-Regiment 36* (*14. Panzer-Division*). He was killed in action in the East on 26 September 1941. The training schedules are from his company.

"Repair and Recovery Services"[11]

The success of the armored division depends greatly not only on the quickness and reliability of its logistics but on the speedy execution of vehicular repair. Without seamlessly functioning vehicle maintenance services, losses of vehicles in war through enemy action, accidents, wear and tear and breakage endanger combat readiness after a few days of movement and combat.

Maintenance services have to be organized and equipped in such a fashion that disabled vehicles are once again available and operational after a short time to the forces in the field. Two prerequisites exist to obtain this goal: repair on the scene to avoid long evacuations and time and swapping components (exchange of parts and modules for others instead of repairing the individual parts).

Maintenance services are responsible for conducting repairs rapidly both day and night, on the spot, under difficult conditions (darkness; moving up repair means in difficult terrain) and under enemy countermeasures. The men of the maintenance services have to place great emphasis on ensuring that disabled vehicles rapidly return to their formations. Their activities, which are so important for their formation, usually take place when the combat elements are resting. It is therefore very important that the proper personnel are selected.

Repair services are conducted by contact teams, maintenance sections and armor maintenance companies. Every tank company has a contact team, as do the battalion and regimental headquarters. It consists of specialists (noncommissioned officer in charge with tank mechanics, tank radio mechanics, engine mechanics) on a team vehicle, a truck for team equipment and motorcycles.

The contact teams need to assure that the repaired vehicles moving out for the attack are secure when moving across the relatively short distance needed to reach the attack zone. Bogging down in the attack deprives the armored fighting vehicle of its greatest protection, namely, its speed.

After the last wave and the motorized rifle formations have crossed the attack zone and direct enemy influence on the battlefield can no longer be expected, the contact teams search out disabled

11. Author's Note: This section is taken from the periodical *Die Wehrmacht*, Vol. 2, Issue 22 of 2 November 1938 (published by the *Oberkommando der Wehrmacht*), 52 ff.

Repair and Recovery Services of a Tank Regiment

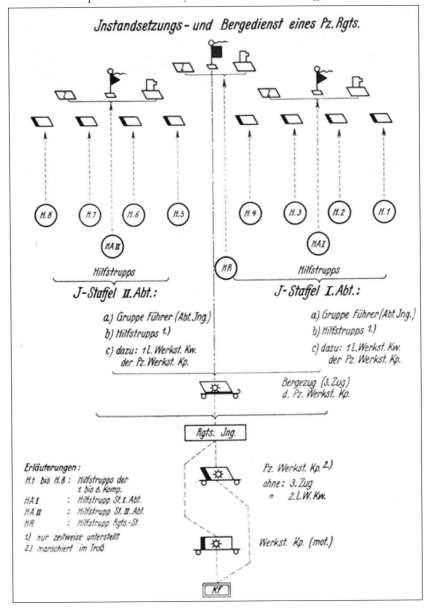

Legend: *Hilfstrupps* = Maintenance (Contact) Teams; *J-Staffel* = *Instandsetzungs-Staffel* = Maintenance Section; *Gruppe Führer* = Group Leader; *dazu: 1 l. Werkst.Kw....* = In addition: 1 light maintenance section of the maintenance company; *Bergezug* = Recovery Platoon; *Erläuterungen* = Legend; *H1* to *H8*: *Hilfstrupp 1* to *Hilfstrupp 8*; *HAI* or *II* = Contact team for the headquarters company of the respective battalion; *nur zeitweise unterstellt* = only attached temporarily; *marschiert im Troß* = Marches with the trains; *Rgts.Ing.* = *Regiments-Ingenieur* = Regiment Engineer; *Pz.Werkst.Kp.* = *Panzer-Werkstatt-Kompanie* = Armor Maintenance Company; *Werkst.Kp. (mot.)* = *Werkstatt-Kompanie (mot)* = Motorized Maintenance Company; *Kf* = *Kraftfahrpark* = Depot.

vehicles in the attack zones of their units. Quickly executable repairs are done on the spot in the field.

Immobilized armored fighting vehicles are towed to a collection point that was designated in the attack order. The assistance teams render all of the disabled armored fighting vehicles on the battlefield mobile or at least towable. Vehicles that can be repaired are not allowed to fall into enemy hands under any circumstances!

When the combat elements move out for the attack, all of the work of the contact teams is stopped. The contact teams are consolidated in the maintenance section of the battalion under its leader (battalion engineer). They are employed by him in accordance with the battalion order for the attack.

Every armor regiment has an armor maintenance company. Each tank battalion has a maintenance section. The contacts teams, which are collocated with their units when road-marching, in rest positions or assembly areas, are consolidated under the command of the leader of the maintenance section during and after the battle.

The command group of the maintenance section consists of the battalion engineer (leader), motorcycle dispatch riders and trucks with repair means or replacement parts with a tank or engine mechanic. Located with the battalion maintenance section is usually a light workshop truck, which is the forward element of the armor maintenance company. The vehicle is outfitted with the tool, devices and replacement parts most needed to eliminate defects of medium magnitude that cannot be repaired by the contact teams. Vehicles that cannot complete the attack to the end, because of battle damage, for instance, move under their own power to the maintenance contact point. The crews of disabled vehicles that are immobilized establish contact with maintenance personnel there. Repairs that can be effected quickly—for example by using individual parts and groups taken off of vehicles more severely damaged—are repaired on the spot.

If a vehicle cannot be made towable, the leader of the maintenance section is notified so that he can arrange for its recovery. The armor maintenance company consists of two maintenance platoons and a recovery platoon.

The maintenance platoons effect repairs that cannot be done by the contact teams, the maintenance sections or the light workshop trucks. To that end, they have specialists (engine mechanics, tank mechanics, vehicle electricians, metalworkers, smiths, mechanics, welders, saddlers, lathe operators, carpenters etc.) and the necessary workshop and equipment vehicles necessary for more comprehensive and difficult work. In addition, they have trucks for replacement parts. Their equipment and machines correspond roughly to those of a workshop in a permanent structure.

The prime movers and trailers of a tank regiment are consolidated in the recovery platoon (3rd Platoon). When road-marching, it is responsible for the recovery of disabled vehicles that cannot be made mobile again on the spot. The recovery platoon follows the combat elements as far as the assembly area. Together with the maintenance sections, it advances along the designated maintenance contact route or in specially designated sectors. In addition, the armor maintenance company has a weapons repair facility and a repair facility for signals equipment.

The regimental engineer accomplishes the same functions for the area of the armor regiment as the battalion engineer does for his battalion. Within the command and control of the division, questions concerning vehicular repair, replacement parts supply and demand, employment and distribution of repair and recovery means, the use of permanent maintenance facilities, etc. is handled by the divisional engineer. Within the command and control of the corps, those questions are handled by the corps engineer.

Replacing track on a *Panzer II*.

Spring 1938: *Hauptmann* Gierga and his 1st Company march out to a swearing-in ceremony. All the way to the left is *Leutnant* Hans Sandrock, who received the Knight's Cross to the Iron Cross on 18 October 1944.

The regimental band on the occasion of a ceremony in the *General-Lutz-Kaserne*.

The first *Panzer IV's* arrive for the regiment at the *General-Lutz-Kaserne*.

The platoon leader's vehicle of the 2nd Platoon of the 8th Company.

The crew of a *Panzer IV*: Commander, gunner, loader, driver and radio operator.

Looking down into the driver's hatch of a *Panzer IV.*

Oberst Walther K. Nehring, the regimental commander. (Courtesy of Christian Nehring)

20 April 1938: *Panzer-Regiment 5* lines up for the 49th birthday celebration of the head of state in Berlin. The *Brandenburger Tor* can be seen in the background.

During the night of 23–24 September, the regiment was alerted as part of the *3. Panzer-Division* and initially dispatched to Ratibor in Upper Silesia. From there, it moved into the *Sudetenland* from 8 to 10 October, returning to Wünsdorf on 22 October. Crossing the Czech border on the morning of 8 October.

An Sd.Kfz. 231 eight-wheeled armored car crosses the border on 8 October.

A *Panzer II* of the regimental headquarters tests the effectiveness of the Czech tank obstacles.

The regiment enters Troppau. Note that the *Panzer I* is on a trailer, probably disabled.

Czech soldiers provide the "German greeting." The men are probably ethnic Germans, who had been conscripted into the Czech Army.

Another view of the entry into Troppau.

Troppau has been elaborately decorated. The banner reads: "We thank our *Führer!*"

Tanks of the 1st Company.

The 2nd Company in Neu-Titschein.

H. Gru. 4
XVI. A. K.
3. Pz. Div.
3. Pz. Brig.

Panzerregiment 5

Bernau b Berlin (vorläufig Wünsdorf [Kr Teltow])

Kommandeur: Oberst Nehring   *Walthn, geb. 15.8.92*   1. 3.37   (6)

Maj. Schaefer				1. 4.36	(66)	1	
Dr. Freiherr von Maffenbach (3t. 2. Pz. Div.)				1. 1.38	(40)	NSt	
von Wilcke				1. 4.38	(3)	11	
Wendenburg				1. 8.38	(42)	4	

				Lt. Ehrhardt	1. 4.37	(405)	5
Hptm. Ritter Edler				Nitfchke	1. 4.37	(934)	2
von Peter				Sandrock	1. 4.37	(1005)	1
(Pz. Abw. Lehrabt.)	1. 4.34	(132)	6	Wiśniewski	1. 4.37	(1261)	8
(E) Moderfohn	1. 4.34	(140)	NSt	Kuhn (Pz. R. 11)	1. 1.38	(397)	6
(E) Littmann	1. 4.34	(525)	St 11	Freiherr von			
Schmidt	1. 7.34	(53)	2	Schlippenbach	1. 1.38	(657)	3
Baffenge	1. 8.35	(15)	3	Müller-Hauff	1. 1.38	(688)	5
Müller	1. 3.37	(8)	8	Schauwecker	1. 1.38	(1046)	7
Gierga	1. 4.37	(17)	1	von Kraufe	1. 1.38	(1102)	4
Oblt. Kühlein	1.10.35	(21)	NAbj	Zorn	1. 1.38	(1561)	4
(W) Kerften	1.10.37	(21)	NSt	Hennig	1. 1.38	(1586)	8
von Oertzen	1. 6.38	(34)	7	Riedefel			
Hofmann	1. 6.38	(133)	NSt	Freiherr zu			
Gierga	1. 6.38	(183)	4	Eifenbach	1. 1.38	(1609)	1
Loffen	1.10.38	(58)	St 11	Köppen	1. 1.38	(1688)	6
Lt. Jarofch-von				Rocholl	Ern. 1. 9.38	(268)	8
Schweder	1. 4.37	(20)	St 1	Großer-			
Grün	1. 4.37	(359)	Abj 11	Schlepps	Ern. 1. 9.38	(421)	2
Stiewe	1. 4.37	(370)	3	Ritfchel	Ern. 1. 9.38	(1449)	7
Moderfohn	1. 4.37	(402)	Abj 1				

Organization of the Regiment
(as of 1 March 1939)
In Accordance with the Table of Organization and Equipment[1]
(Minus the Wheeled Elements and the Maintenance Company)

---

1. Author's Note: Jentz, *Die deutsche Panzertruppe*, Vol. 1, 56–62. Translator's Note: In German, the TO&E was known as a *Kriegsstärkennachweisung* and abbreviated as *KStN*.

4. Until the End of August 1939

The command positions were occupied as follows on 1 March 1939:

Panzer-Regiment 5
Commander: *Oberst* Nehring

1st Battalion
Commander: *Major* Schaeffer
1st Company: *Hauptmann* Gierga
2nd Company: *Hauptmann* Schmidt
3rd Company: *Hauptmann* Bassenge
4th Company: *Major* Wendenburg

2nd Battalion
Commander: *Major* von Wilcke
5th Company: *Leutnant* Ehrhardt

6th Company: *Hauptmann Ritter Edler* von Peter
7th Company: *Oberleutnant* von Oertzen
8th Company: *Hauptmann* Müller

The Tables of Organization and Equipment established the official organization, personnel authorizations, types and numbers of weapons and types and numbers of vehicles and other major items of equipment.

Unfortunately, there are no lists of actual "on-hand" numbers of tanks for the regiment from 1935 to August 1939. As a result of the rapid expansion of the army and the personnel detachments associated with it, the companies of the regiment rarely had the same numbers or types of vehicles. It was rare for them to reach authorized levels. The TO&E listed here should therefore only be used as a guide.

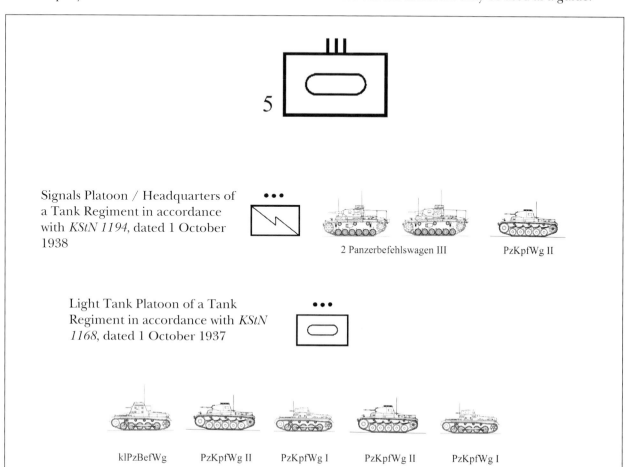

Signals Platoon / Headquarters of a Tank Regiment in accordance with *KStN 1194*, dated 1 October 1938

2 Panzerbefehlswagen III

PzKpfWg II

Light Tank Platoon of a Tank Regiment in accordance with *KStN 1168*, dated 1 October 1937

klPzBefWg   PzKpfWg II   PzKpfWg I   PzKpfWg II   PzKpfWg I

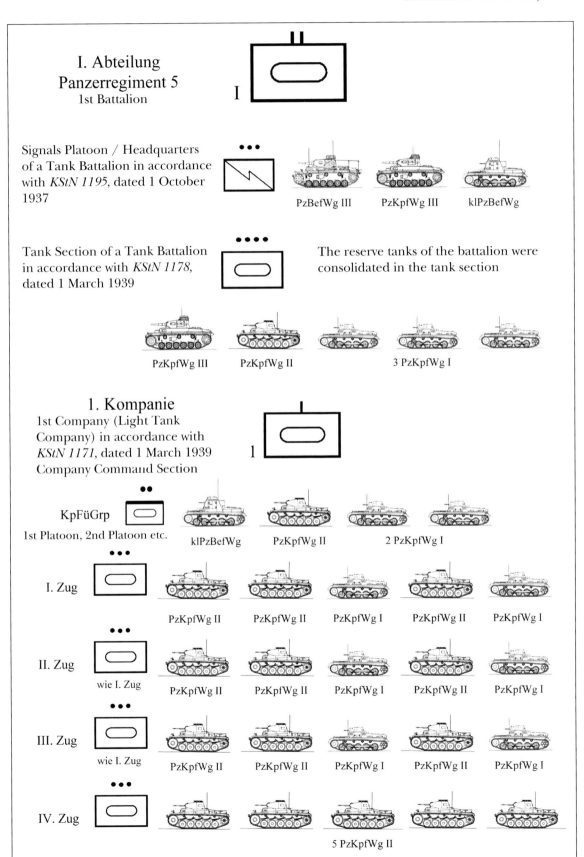

I. Abteilung Panzerregiment 5
1st Battalion

Signals Platoon / Headquarters of a Tank Battalion in accordance with *KStN 1195*, dated 1 October 1937

PzBefWg III   PzKpfWg III   klPzBefWg

Tank Section of a Tank Battalion in accordance with *KStN 1178*, dated 1 March 1939

The reserve tanks of the battalion were consolidated in the tank section

PzKpfWg III   PzKpfWg II   3 PzKpfWg I

1. Kompanie
1st Company (Light Tank Company) in accordance with *KStN 1171*, dated 1 March 1939
Company Command Section

KpFüGrp
1st Platoon, 2nd Platoon etc.

klPzBefWg   PzKpfWg II   2 PzKpfWg I

I. Zug

PzKpfWg II   PzKpfWg II   PzKpfWg I   PzKpfWg II   PzKpfWg I

II. Zug
wie I. Zug

PzKpfWg II   PzKpfWg II   PzKpfWg I   PzKpfWg II   PzKpfWg I

III. Zug
wie I. Zug

PzKpfWg II   PzKpfWg II   PzKpfWg I   PzKpfWg II   PzKpfWg I

IV. Zug

5 PzKpfWg II

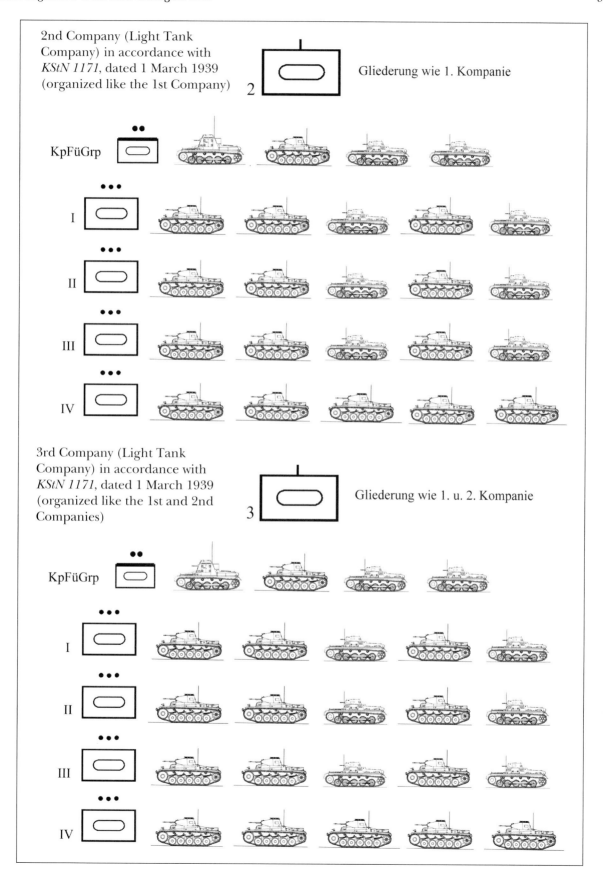

2nd Company (Light Tank Company) in accordance with *KStN 1171*, dated 1 March 1939 (organized like the 1st Company)

Gliederung wie 1. Kompanie

KpFüGrp

I

II

III

IV

3rd Company (Light Tank Company) in accordance with *KStN 1171*, dated 1 March 1939 (organized like the 1st and 2nd Companies)

Gliederung wie 1. u. 2. Kompanie

KpFüGrp

I

II

III

IV

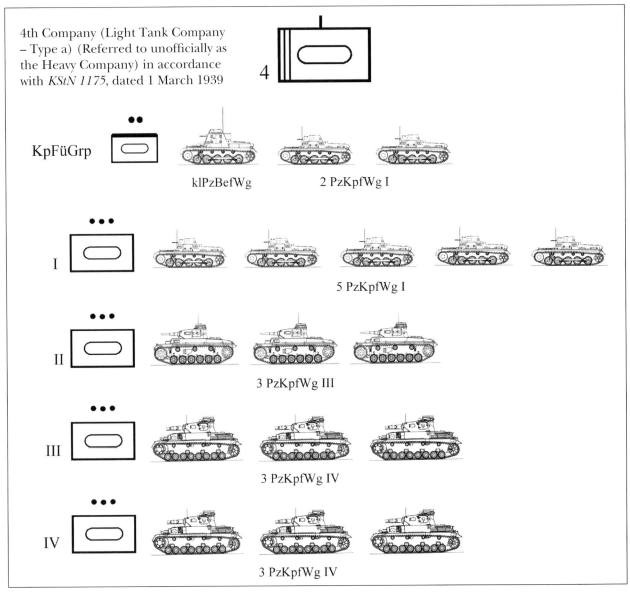

4th Company (Light Tank Company – Type a) (Referred to unofficially as the Heavy Company) in accordance with *KStN 1175*, dated 1 March 1939

4

KpFüGrp

klPzBefWg　　　　2 PzKpfWg I

I　　　5 PzKpfWg I

II　　　3 PzKpfWg III

III　　　3 PzKpfWg IV

IV　　　3 PzKpfWg IV

Crew locations in a *Panzer IV*: 1 = Tank Commander; 2 = Gunner; 3 = Loader; 4 = Radio Operator/ Hull Machine-Gun Operator; 5 = Driver

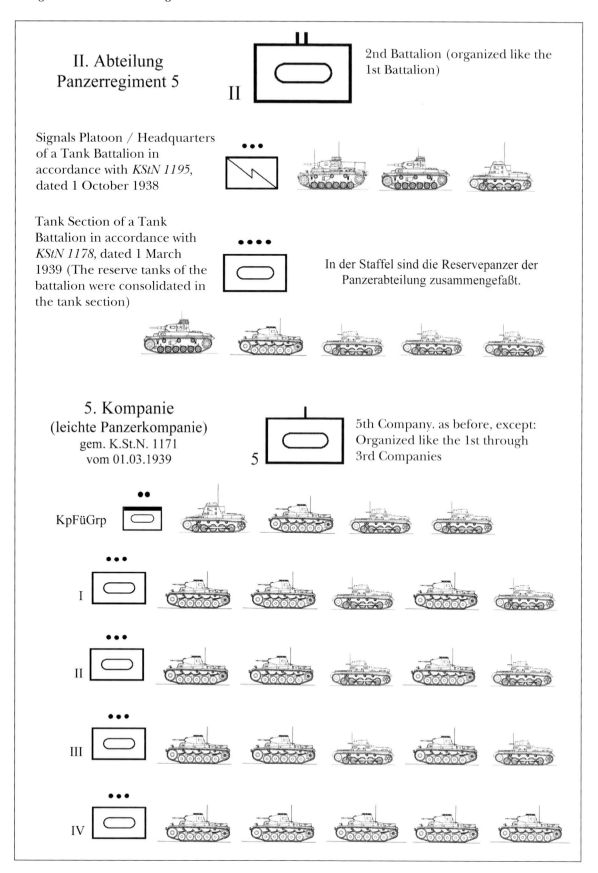

II. Abteilung Panzerregiment 5

II — 2nd Battalion (organized like the 1st Battalion)

Signals Platoon / Headquarters of a Tank Battalion in accordance with *KStN 1195*, dated 1 October 1938

Tank Section of a Tank Battalion in accordance with *KStN 1178*, dated 1 March 1939 (The reserve tanks of the battalion were consolidated in the tank section)

In der Staffel sind die Reservepanzer der Panzerabteilung zusammengefaßt.

5. Kompanie (leichte Panzerkompanie) gem. K.St.N. 1171 vom 01.03.1939

5 — 5th Company. as before, except: Organized like the 1st through 3rd Companies

KpFüGrp

I

II

III

IV

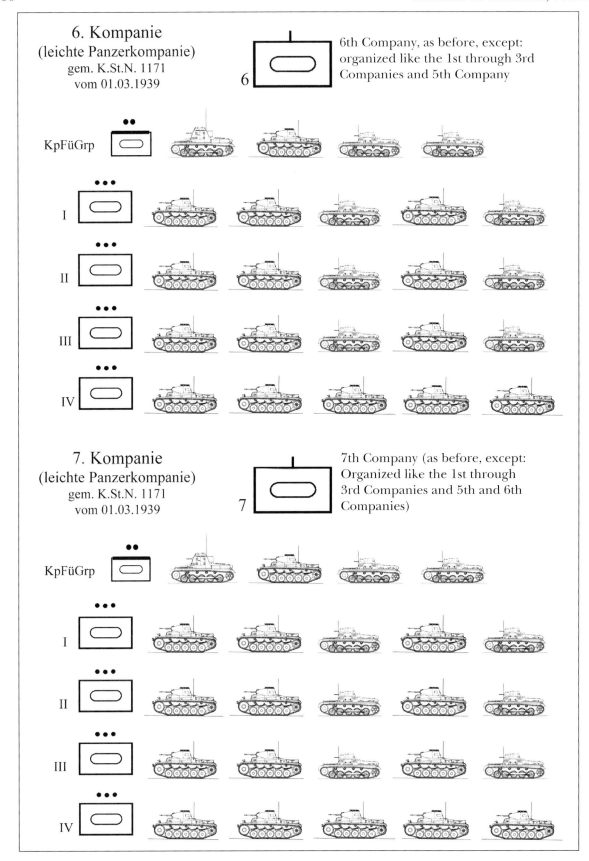

6. Kompanie
(leichte Panzerkompanie)
gem. K.St.N. 1171
vom 01.03.1939

6th Company, as before, except: organized like the 1st through 3rd Companies and 5th Company

KpFüGrp

I

II

III

IV

7. Kompanie
(leichte Panzerkompanie)
gem. K.St.N. 1171
vom 01.03.1939

7th Company (as before, except: Organized like the 1st through 3rd Companies and 5th and 6th Companies)

KpFüGrp

I

II

III

IV

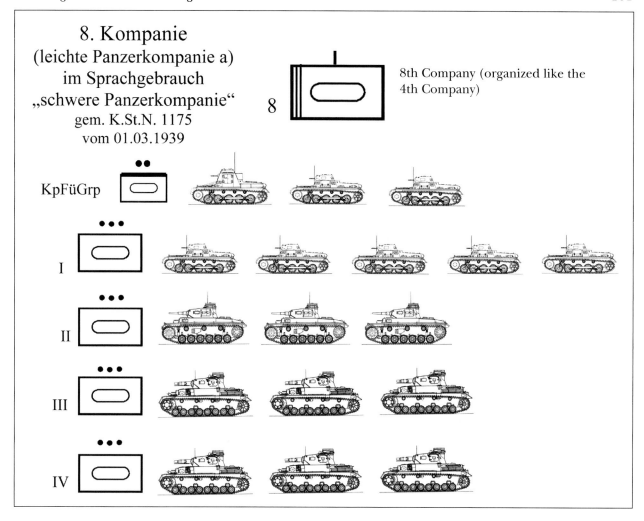

8. Kompanie
(leichte Panzerkompanie a)
im Sprachgebrauch
„schwere Panzerkompanie"
gem. K.St.N. 1175
vom 01.03.1939

8th Company (organized like the 4th Company)

KpFüGrp

I

II

III

IV

The authorized strength of a tank battalion was as follows:

  5 Small Command & Control Tanks
  1 *Panzer III* Command & Control Tank
34 *Panzer I's*
46 *Panzer II's*
  5 *Panzer III's*
  6 *Panzer IV's*
97 tanks per battalion

The entire regiment had the following number of authorized tanks:

11 Small Command & Control Tanks
  4 *Panzer III* Command & Control Tanks
70 *Panzer I's*
95 *Panzer II's*
10 *Panzer III's*
12 *Panzer IV's*
202 tanks in the regiment

15 March 1939: Difficult crossing of the Lückendorf Pass

Until the start of the war in September, no new armored formations were established in 1939. As a result of the hasty expansion of the military, it was intended to give the formations time to develop cohesiveness.

For the first two months of 1939, the daily regimen was routine. On 10 March, however, the 1st Battalion was alerted. The 2nd Battalion, which had just been re-established, was not yet combat ready as a result of the personnel it had to give up to form *Panzer-Regiment 36* in Schweinfurt. The situation was similar in the division's other tank regiment, *Panzer-Regiment 6*, in Neuruppin. As a result, only the *I./Panzer-regiment 5* and the *II./Panzer-Regiment 6* were loaded on trains and sent to the Königsbrück Training Area.

Both of the battalions were placed under the command of *Oberstleutnant* Rothenburg, forming the *ad hoc Regiment Rothenburg*. On 15 March, the regiment marched as part of the division into what remained of Czechoslovakia, Bohemia and Moravia. The winter weather was extreme and the crossing of the Lückendorf Pass in the Lausitz Range demanded the utmost of drivers.

The march objective was Prague. Rothenburg was able to report his regiment had reached the city on 16 March. On 17 March, a pass-in-review was conducted for the commander of the *3. Panzer-Division* on the *Wenzelplatz*. Two days later, on 19 March, another parade was held for the Commander-in-Chief of *Heeresgruppe 3, General* von Blaskowitz.

Parade on the *Wenzelplatz* in Prague. *Feldwebel* Jäger carries the standard of the 1st Battalion.

For the reunification of the *Sudetenland* with Germany, Hitler had created a medal on 18 October commemorating the event ("Medal Commemorating 1 October 1938"). It was cast in bronze, with the front side having a symbolic portrayal of the acceptance of the *Sudetenland* into the *Reich*. The reverse bore the date of "1 October 1938" and the phrase "One People—One *Reich*—One *Führer*" along the edge. The ribbon was in the Sudeten German colors of black-red-black.

Based on a directive issued on 1 May, the medal was also to be awarded for those who participated in the occupation of the rest of Czechoslovakia. For those who already had the medal, a "Prague" clasp was also created, which was worn on the medal's ribbon. The clasp bore a relief of the Prague Castle.

The soldiers of *Panzer-Regiment 5* who were eligible for one or both awards did not receive them until after the campaign in Poland had concluded, when the events in questions were nearly a year old and had almost been forgotten as a result of the war.

The Medal Commemorating 1 October 1938. Obverse on left, reverse on right. The final medals were awarded by 31 December 1940. By then, some 1,162,617 medals had been awarded, along with 134,563 clasps.

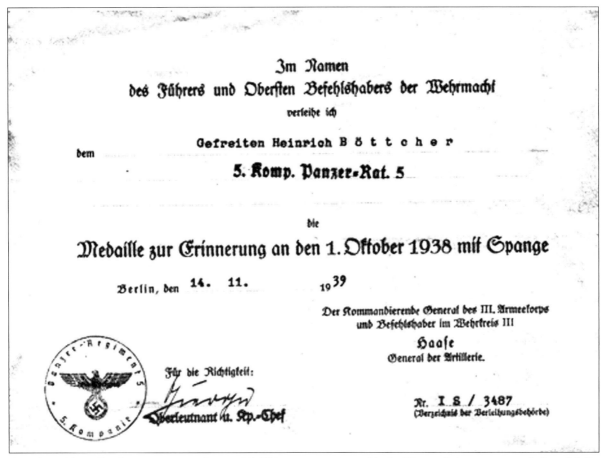

Im Namen
des Führers und Obersten Befehlshabers der Wehrmacht
verleihe ich

dem

Gefreiten Heinrich B ö t t c h e r
5. Komp. Panzer-Rgt. 5

die

Medaille zur Erinnerung an den 1. Oftober 1938 mit Spange

Berlin, den   14. 11.   19 39

Der Kommandierende General des III. Armeekorps
und Befehlshaber im Wehrkreis III

Haase
General der Artillerie.

Für die Richtigkeit:

Oberleutnant u. Kp.-Chef

Nr. I S / 3487
(Verzeichnis der Verleihungsbehörde)

Award certificate for the commemoration medal. This one, complete with the "Prague" clasp, was awarded to *Gefreiter* Heinrich Böttcher of the 5th Company.

On 20 April, the regiment participated in the *Führer* parade in Berlin. On 26 April, the 1st Battalion received a new commander, *Major* von Lewinski. The previous commander, *Major* Schaeffer, was transferred to the *Panzer-Lehr-Regiment*.

From 7 to 18 May, there was gunnery training at the Camp Senne Training Area.

Noncommissioned officers and enlisted personnel were entitled to wear a marksmanship lanyard after fulfilling certain conditions during gunnery training.

The lanyard was awarded in 12 levels. For levels I through IV, the wreath surrounding the *Panzer I* under the national insignia was composed of tank track. It was made out of aluminum, with the wreath being relatively small. For the remaining levels of the award, the wreath was composed of Oak Leaves. For levels V through VIII, the award was also cast in aluminum, but the wreath was wider. For the remaining levels, the award was cast in a gold color. The individual levels were represented by main-gun rounds that hung from the bottom of the cord. For instance, Level I had no rounds; Level II, one round; Level III, two rounds; and Level IV, three rounds. The remaining levels were represented analogously.

Levels I to IV.

Levels V to XII.

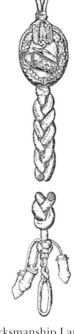

Marksmanship Lanyard for Armored Personnel, Level XII.

2 June 1939: Parade for Hitler and Prince Regent Paul in Berlin. *Panzer IV's* of the regiment move past the reviewing stand.

In May, tactical training was conducted at the Döberitz Training Area. While there, the commander of the 2nd Battalion was also the acting regimental commander. The frequent absence of *Oberst* Nehring at the time was due to his planned transfer to the *XIX. Armee-Korps (mot)* as its Chief-of-Staff.[12] On 2 June, the regiment participated in a parade held for Hitler and the prince regent of Yugoslavia, Paul. The parade served as an impressive demonstration of German military might in a time of increasing international tensions.

12. Author's Note: Nehring, 105.

The "Legion Condor" Tank Badge. It was awarded to
tankers who had volunteered and participated in the
Spanish Civil War.

On 6 June, there were ceremonies in Berlin celebrating the return of the German participants in the Spanish Civil War of 1936–39. Tankers of the regiment, who had participated in those operations, were awarded the "Spanish Cross" and the Tank Badge of the Condor Legion. The former was worn on the right chest, and the latter on the left. All of the award documents for the "Spanish Cross" are dated 6 June.

The summer was marked by a rotation at the Bergen Training Area from 15 to 30 June. That was followed by an alert on 20 August and movement to the Groß-Born Training Area in Pomerania. It was the staging area for the *XIX. Armee-Korps (mot)*, to which the *3. Panzer-Division* had been assigned. Reports concerning incidents along the eastern borders of the *Reich* caused a depressed mood among the troops in light of the increasing danger of war.

The dramatic increase in tension in the political situation soon brought the certainty that operations would be carried out against Poland. On 25 August, the regiment occupied an assembly area southeast of Preußisch-Friedland and prepared to attack on 31 August.

August 1939: The 1st Battalion's assembly area. The men pass the time in an uncertain situation.

5. Overview of Chapter 2: *Panzer-Regiment 5* from 1936 to August 1939

February–April 1936	Movement to the Camp Senne Training Area in conjunction with the German occupation of the demilitarized Rhineland
October 1936	Detachments to *Panzer-Regiment 8* in Zossen
April 1937	The regiment's battalions receive their standards
Summer 1937	Issue of the *Panzer II*
October 1937	Detachments to *Panzer-Regiment 15* in Sagen and the Putlos Gunnery School
13 October 1937	*Oberst* Nehring assumes command of the regiment
Spring 1938	Issue of the *Panzer III* and *Panzer IV*
October 1938	Entry into the *Sudetenland* by the *3. Panzer-Division*
October–November 1938	Detachments to *Panzer-Regiment 36* in Schweinfurt
March 1939	The 1st Battalion participates in the march into Bohemia and Moravia as part of *Regiment Rothenburg*
August 1939	The regiment is moved as part of the division to Pomerania and the Groß-Born Training Area
31 August 1939	Preparations for attack along the eastern German border

Beginning of 1939: The command and control *Panzer I* (*kleiner Panzerbefehlswagen*).

15 March 1939: Moving through the snowed-over Erz Mountains into the rest of Czechoslovakia in the Zittau area.

A *Panzer II* of the 1st Company in front of the main train station in Prague.

19 March 1939: Parade in Prague for *General* Blaskowitz, the Commander-in-Chief of *Heeresgruppe 3*. A *Panzer II* of the 1st Battalion moves past the reviewing stand with the battalion standard.

The *Wenzelplatz* in Prague. Parade in front of *Reich* Protector Neurath, *Generaloberst* von Brauchitsch and *Generalleutnant* Geyr von Schweppenburg, the commander of the *3. Panzer-Division.*

Panzer II's of the 1st Company in the streets of Prague. A happy young potential recruit takes temporary command.

The regimental band plays an impromptu concert in the staging area of the 4th Company of the regiment.

2 June 1939: Parade for *Reich* Chancellor Hitler and the prince regent of Yugoslavia, Paul. The color guard of one of the regiment's battalions moves past the reviewing stand. In the foreground, the regimental band has taken up position.

CHAPTER 3

Panzer-Regiment 5 in the Campaign in Poland, 1939

1. Organization and Strength of *Panzer-Regiment 5* for the Campaign

After the mobilization, the 1st Battalion gave up its 3rd Company and the 2nd Battalion its 7th Company to help form a tank training and replacement detachment, *Panzer-Ersatz-Abteilung 5*.[1]

1. Author's Note: Jentz, *Die deutsche Panzertruppe*, Vol. I, 88.

After those two companies were detached, the regiment had six tank companies at its disposal for the start of the campaign in Poland on 1 September 1939. The chart on the next page illustrates the numbers and types of tanks on hand.[2] The *Panzer I's* and *II's* bore the brunt of the fighting, with the *Panzer III's* and *IV's* providing a reinforcing role.

For the campaign, the *Panzer-Lehr-Abteilung* was attached to the regiment, forming a 3rd Battalion.[3] Since the last peacetime commander of the regiment, *Oberst* Nehring, was summoned away to perform his mobilization duties as Chief-of-Staff of the *XIX. Armee Korps (mot)*, the regiment was commanded during the campaign by the commander of the *Panzer-Lehr-Regiment, Oberstleutnant* Conze.[4]

2. Author's Note: Jentz, 90.

3. Author's Note: Kampe, *Wünsdorf*, 41.

4. Author's Note: Ritgen, *Die Schulen der Panzertruppen des Heeres*, 220.

Oberstleutnant Conze led the regiment in Poland.

Tank Type	On-hand Strength of PR5 on 1 September 1939 with 6 Companies	Authorized strength for the Regiment (minus the 3rd and 7th Companies) in accordance with the TO&E on 1 September 1939
klPzBefWg	8	9
PzBefWg III		4
Panzerkampfwagen I	63	54
Panzerkampfwagen II	77	65
Panzerkampfwagen III	3	10
Panzerkampfwagen IV	9	12
Summe	160	154

Prior to the start of the campaign, the vehicles of the regiment were marked with large white crosses to serve as nationality markers while at the Groß-Born Training Area. The crosses proved to be disadvantageous, since they offered the enemy a good aiming point for his antitank weapons. As a result, the crosses were blackened out later by most of the crews.

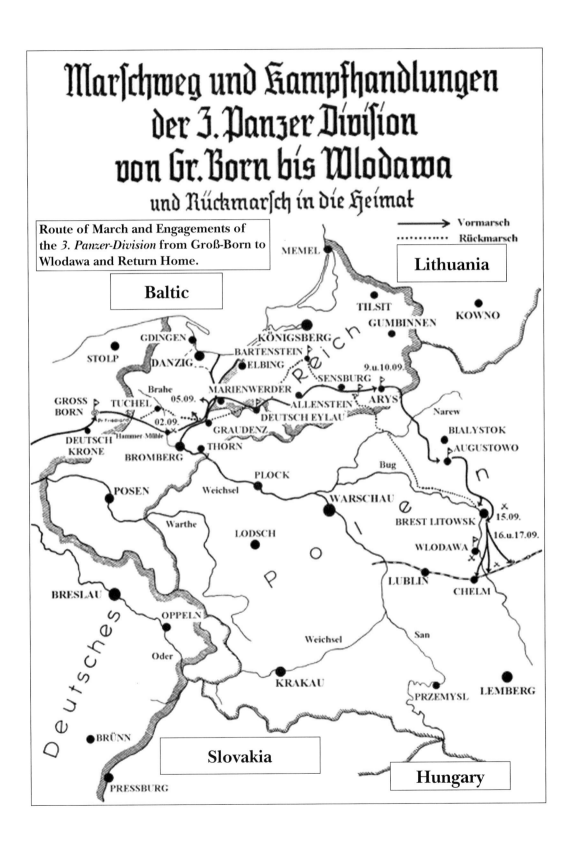

Marschweg und Kampfhandlungen der 3. Panzer Division von Gr. Born bis Wlodawa und Rückmarsch in die Heimat

Route of March and Engagements of the *3. Panzer-Division* from Groß-Born to Wlodawa and Return Home.

2. Combat Operations from 1 to 21 September 1939

The German head of state appealed to the armed forces at the start of the war on 1 September 1939 as follows:[5]

To the Armed Forces!

The Polish state has turned down the peaceful negotiation of neighborly relations that had been sought by me; instead, it has appealed to weapons.

The Germans in Poland have been persecuted with bloody terror, driven from hearth and home. A number of border violations—unacceptable for a major power—have proven that the Poles are no longer willing to honor the borders of the *Reich*. In order to bring this insanity to an end, no other means are left to us except to now use force against force.

The German Armed Forces will conduct the fight for the honor and right to survive of the newly resurrected German people with tough decisiveness.

I expect that every soldier will fulfill his duty to the utmost, conscious of the great, perpetual tradition of German soldiery.

Remain conscious, always and everywhere, that you are representatives of a National Socialist Greater Germany!

Long live our people and our *Reich*!

Adolf Hitler

Berlin, 1 September 1939

5. Author's Note: Heller, *Das war der Krieg in Polen*, 22.

An die Wehrmacht!

Der polnische Staat hat die von mir erstrebte friedliche Regelung nachbarlicher Beziehungen verweigert; er hat statt dessen an die Waffen appelliert.

Die Deutschen in Polen werden mit blutigem Terror verfolgt, von Haus und Hof vertrieben. Eine Reihe von für eine Großmacht unerträglichen Grenzverletzungen beweist, daß die Polen nicht mehr gewillt sind, die deutsche Reichsgrenze zu achten. Um diesem wahnwitzigen Treiben ein Ende zu bereiten, bleibt mir kein anderes Mittel, als von jetzt ab Gewalt gegen Gewalt zu setzen.

Die deutsche Wehrmacht wird den Kampf um die Ehre und die Lebensrechte des wiederauferstandenen deutschen Volkes mit harter Entschlossenheit führen.

Ich erwarte, daß jeder Soldat eingedenk der großen Tradition des ewigen deutschen Soldatentums seine Pflicht bis zum Letzten erfüllen wird.

Bleibt Euch stets und in allen Lagen bewußt, daß Ihr die Repräsentanten des nationalsozialistischen Großdeutschlands seid!

Es lebe unser Volk und unser Reich!

Adolf Hitler

Berlin, den 1. September 1939

The *3. Panzer-Division*, under the command of *Generalleutnant Freiherr* Geyr von Schweppenburg, was part of the *XIX. Armee-Korps (mot)* of *General der Panzertruppen* Guderian. In addition to the *3. Panzer-Division*, the corps consisted of the *2. Infanterie-Division (mot)*,[6] the *20. Infanterie-Division (mot)*[7] and the *23. Infanterie-Division* (corps reserve).[8] As already mentioned, the Chief-of-Staff was *Oberst i.G.* Nehring. The mission of the division and, hence, the tank regiment, was the elimination of Polish forces in the corridor that existed between Germany and its eastern province of East Prussia.

---

6. Translator's Note: This division later became the *12. Panzer-Division*, fighting exclusively in the East after its reorganization and redesignation.

7. Translator's Note: This division later became the *20. Panzer-Grenadier-Division*, fighting exclusively in the East after its reorganization and redesignation.

8. Translator's Note: This division later became the *26. Panzer-Division*, fighting with distinction in Italy at the end of the war.

The *3. Panzer-Division*, having the most combat power of the corps, was employed as the main effort, spearheaded by the *3. Panzer-Brigade*, consisting of the regiment and its sister formation, *Panzer-Regiment 6*. The division initially advanced into the area of the Tuchel Heath.

The attack started around 0445 hours on 1 September. The commanding general moved along with the regiment in a *Schützenpanzerwagen*[9] that had been converted to a command and control vehicle.[10]

The regiment was employed on the right, with *Panzer-Regiment 6* on the left. Together, they took the objective of the day, the Brahe River, which flows from the south to the north through the Tuchel Heath, by noon. It was a scorching hot day. By doing

---

9. Translator's Note: *SPW* = Armored personnel carrier. This was the medium variant, the *Sd.Kfz. 251*.

10. Author's Note: Kurowski, *Die Geschichte des Panzer-Regiment 5*, 14

A *Panzer II* of the 2nd Battalion after the fighting of 2 September.

so, the *3. Panzer-Brigade*, to which the divisional re-connaissance battalion, *Aufklärungs-Abteilung 3 (mot)*, had been attached, was 30 kilometers deep in enemy territory, driving a wedge into the enemy field army. Attacks by a Polish cavalry brigade charging on horseback with drawn sabers were bloodily repulsed. Guderian ordered the division to cross the Brahe that same afternoon and, by evening, a bridgehead had been formed on the far side of the river.

A critical situation arose for a short while on the morning of 2 September as the result of Polish counterattacks, but the situation could be mastered. The attack east was then continued. The lead elements of the regiment ran into enemy artillery positions and eliminated them. Despite brave Polish resistance and not inconsiderable friendly losses, the *3. Panzer-Division* broke open the front of the Polish field army in the corridor time and again.

The regiment advanced as far as Graudenz by 4 September, advancing along the sandy soil and through dark woods. The city was only a few kilometers from the frontier with East Prussia along the Vistula. That meant that the encirclement of the Polish forces in the northern part of the corridor was only a question of time. The division was subjected to strong Polish counterattacks through the afternoon of 4 September, with enemy forces numbering upwards of 20,000.

Command of the *3. Panzer-Brigade* was transferred to *Generalmajor* Stumpff that same day due to the sudden illness of *Oberst* Rothenburg.

The other divisions of the corps had caught up in the meantime, and they undertook the task of completing the encirclement of the Polish corridor army. It was the first pocket battle of the Second World War, and *Panzer-Regiment 5* had played a major role in its success.

Starting on 7 September, the formations of the *3. Panzer-Division* were moved into the eastern portion of East Prussia so as to conduct a new thrust south from there. Three hundred and eighty kilometers were covered in the space of three days. The units marched under nice weather through Marienwerder, Deutsch-Eylau, Allenstein and as far as the training area at Arys. Guderian requested that his corps swing wide out to the east of the *3. Armee*, so as to take the Bug River at Brest-Litowsk and thus enveloping the enemy field armies in eastern Poland. The recommendation was approved by the German Army High Command.

A Polish tank knocked out on the way to Brest-Litowsk. It is a World War I–era Renault FT 17/18 light tank.

Firing position of the division's *Artillerie-Regiment 75*. The artillery piece is a *15-cm sFH 18*.

During the night of 10–12 September, the lead elements of the division crossed the frontier between East Prussia and Poland with the objective of taking Brest-Litowsk. After crossing the Narew, the division stormed south, encountering little resistance.

The tanks interdicted the Brest-Litowsk–Bialystok rail line on 12 September, stopping all rail traffic. The advance on Brest-Litowsk was continued the following day.

The regiment, along with the reconnaissance battalion and a battery of artillery (*3./Artillerie-Regiment 75*) were east of the city by the afternoon of 14 September in an effort to encircle it. The infantry followed and closed.

On 15 September, the division attacked the fortress from the east. Working together with the *20. Infanterie-Division (mot)* advancing from the north, the lead elements of the *3. Panzer-Division* entered the city. While the motorized infantry division fought for the citadel, which did not fall until 17 September, the *3. Panzer-Division* was pulled out of the fighting so as to continue advancing south along the Bug. This time, the regiment and the reconnaissance battalion

formed the spearhead of the division. Impeding the advance was the fact that the unimproved road network had been softened up the previous few days by rain.

When the armored cars of *Aufklärungs-Abteilung 3 (mot)* encountered energetic resistance towards noon on 16 September, *Hauptmann* Schmidt's 2nd Company was brought forward to attack by the battalion commander, *Major* Wendenburg. Schmidt had 19 operational tanks. Combat engineers mounted the vehicles. Moving rapidly, the tanks entered the enemy positions, breaking the resistance. Horse columns were scattered, vehicles went up in flames and antitank guns were destroyed. The advance was continued during the night of 16–17 September. The marshy terrain and thick woods slowed down the advance. The 4th Company took over the lead.

As it turned first light on 17 September, the 1st Battalion was in the Wlodawa area along the Bug, 70 kilometers south of Brest-Litowsk. The battalion blew up rail lines and bridges there, which cut off the enemy from withdrawing across the Bug. At that point, fuel ran low and the 1st Battalion had

Fuel has arrived. The tanks top off using 20-liter fuel canisters.

to transition to an all-round defense. The division's motorcycle infantry battalion, *Kradschützen-Bataillon 3*, then entered Wlodawa from the north. The city fell that morning. After an unsuccessful immediate counterattack, the Poles withdrew to the thick woods to the south of the city. Patrols from the 4th Company were feeling their way farther south, when fuel arrived that afternoon. With the fuel, the entire 1st Battalion could move out again.

On 18 September, the division was far ahead of the other formations of the corps. It had covered the most ground of all German divisions during the campaign. At noon on 18 September, the attack was continued in the direction of Chelm, which was also attacked at the same time from the south by the lead elements of the *XVIII. Armee-Korps*. The attack to take Chelm encountered strong resistance. Only patrols from the motorcycle infantry battalion succeeded in reaching the outskirts of the city. By then, the division had offensively advanced some 300 kilometers south since crossing the East Prussian border. Contrary to what was reported in the Armed Forces Daily Report, the forces of *Heeresgruppe Nord* and *Heeresgruppe Süd*[11] did not link up at Chelm.[12]

The *3. Panzer-Division* issued orders to pull back to Wlodawa. On 17 September, the Soviet Union had attacked Poland from the east. As a result, all of the German forces east of the Bug pulled back to the west in accordance with the secret protocols of the German-Soviet Union Non-Aggression Pact.

After the division had assembled in the Wlodawa area, it started pulling back to Brest-Litowsk on 21 September. On 22 September, there was a combined German-Soviet parade. Following that, the division marched back to the area around Bartenstein in East Prussia, reaching it on 23 September. On 26 September, the divisions of the corps were released from attachment and the corps reverted to being strictly headquarters elements without assigned forces.[13]

Isolated fighting continued against Polish remnants until 5 October before the fighting was finally over.

---

11. Translator's Note: Field Army Group North and South, respectively.

12. Author's Note: *Geschichte der 3. Panzer-Division*, 35.

13. Author's Note: *Geschichte der 3. Panzer-Division*, 36.

3. Lessons Learned

The success registered during the campaign in Poland was due in decisive measure to the armored forces that Guderian had created. The fighting in Poland had been the fledgling force's baptism of fire. From a warfare perspective, it meant the dawning of a new era. What had been hinted at in the Great War had become certainty: The decisive role on the battlefield had transitioned from the infantry to the armored forces.

The massive success of the German forces in only four weeks against a numerically equal opponent and with minimal friendly losses was unique in the history of warfare.[14] It was mostly due to the *Panzertruppe*, in conjunction with the *Luftwaffe*. The latter had rapidly established air superiority and then supported the

armored forces on the ground, enabling their rapid movement.

The doctrines established for the *Panzertruppe* had proven themselves: The armored forces reached their full potential when they were cut loose from the foot-marching infantry, consolidated in large-scale formations and then attacked long-range objectives. All other branches needed to be represented in those armored formations, however, since the tanks were in need of their support. It was also important that those other branches be able to keep pace with the tanks when moving cross country.

Exploiting its firepower, armor and maneuverability, the *Panzertruppe* was in a position to effectively attack the enemy in his deep flank and rear, ultimately enveloping him. As a result, it was

---

14. Author's Note: Nehring, 153.

In the fighting that destroyed this *Panzer I*, *Panzerschütze* Bader of the 2nd Battalion was killed.

capable of being employed in a decisive manner at the operational level.

Although the *Panzertruppe* had acquitted itself well in the campaign, it had not encountered armored forces to any great extent. Finally, it was determined that the tank regiments needed more armored vehicles outfitted with main guns as opposed to machine guns or automatic cannon. Above all, the *Panzer I* had proven to be too weak.

The average age of those killed in the campaign was 24. When looking at casualty lists, it is also striking how high the percentage of noncommissioned officers and officers was, almost one third.

4. The Beginning of October 1939 to the Beginning of May 1940: Between the Campaign in Poland and the Campaign in the West

On 1 October 1939, the *3. Panzer-Division* left its assigned billets in East Prussia. Deserving officers, noncommissioned officers and enlisted personnel received the Iron Cross, which had been reinstituted on 1 September, as a reward for their bravery. The first wound badges were also issued. At the time, the Tank Assault Badge did not yet exist.

The tanks and other tracked vehicles were loaded on ships at Pillau and shipped home that way to help

Panzer II's and *IV's* after the campaign in Poland. For the most part, efforts have been made to eliminate the large white crosses.

Im Kampf zur Befreiung deutschen Bodens im Osten fiel am 2. September an der Brahe im draufgängerischen Panzerangriff der

Leutnant

Ernſt v. Krauſe

Seine frische, schwungvolle Art und seine vorbildliche Kameradschaft werden dem Regiment unvergessen bleiben.

Conze

Oberſtlt. unð Führer eines Panzer-Regiments

An obituary notice taken out in a local newspaper by the acting commander of the regiment, *Oberstleutnant* Conze, for one of his officers who had been killed in the fighting. The text reads: "*Leutnant* Ernst von Krause was killed in the struggle to liberate German soil in the east in an aggressive tank attack along the Brahe on 2 September. His upbeat and jaunty manner and his exemplary comradeship will never be forgotten by the regiment. Conze. *Oberstleutnant* and Acting Commander of a Tank Regiment."

reduce wear and tear.[15] The regiment returned to its peacetime garrisons and was enthusiastically greeted by the local populace. As with the other garrisons of the division, a victory parade was held on 5 October in Wünsdorf. This was followed by several changes in command. The division commander, von Schweppenburg, transferred command to *Generalmajor* Stumpff, the former commander of the *3. Panzer-Brigade*, for health reasons. The new commander of the *3. Panzer-Brigade* was *Oberst* Kühn, the former commander of the Armor School.[16] *Oberstleutnant* Conze, who had held acting command of the regiment during the campaign in Poland, handed over the reins of command to *Oberst Freiherr* von Funck on 15 October. Von Funck had previously

been the military attaché at the German embassy in Lisbon.[17]

On 29 November, the troop elements of the *3. Panzer-Division* left their garrisons again. This time, they headed west. The division occupied an assembly area in the Osnabrück-Glandorf-Warendorf area. The troop elements were largely billeted in farm houses; the tanks were in concealed positions in barns or farmyards. For Christmas 1939, married personnel were allowed to take leave; single men had to remain with their units.

In February 1940, the division found itself on the march again. It crossed the Rhine at Duisburg and reached its operational area for the Western Front, with assembly areas around Krefeld and Viersen. The time was spent in combat training at the Trar Training Area, plus drill and ceremonies, gunnery training and firing, formations, night marches, test alerts and maintenance.

---

15. Author's Note: *Geschichte der 3. Panzer-Division*, 37.

16. Author's Note: He was killed in 1944 as a *General der Panzertruppen* and the head of Armed Forces Motorization during a bombing raid on Berlin.

17. Author's Note: *Geschichte der 3. Panzer-Division*, 37.

In expectation of the campaign in the West, intensive training was conducted in water crossings with vehicles. In this case, a *Panzerbefehlswagen III* crosses a creek by means of the bridge from an armored bridge layer.

5. Overview

Date	Activity
August 1939	Reassignment of two companies to form *Panzer-Ersatz-Abteilung 5*
1 September 1939	Start of the campaign in Poland. *Oberstleutnant* Conze is given acting command of the regiment.
1–5 September 1939	Battle of envelopment against the Polish corridor army
7–10 September 1939	March of the regiment as part of the division through East Prussia
10–15 September 1939	Advance from East Prussia to the south in the direction of Brest-Litowsk
16–17 September 1939	Continuation of the attack in the direction of Wlodawa, approximately 70 kilometers south of Brest-Litowsk.
18 September 1939	Attack of the division into the Chelm area, approximately 120 kilometers south of Brest-Litowsk, signaling the furthest movement of all German divisions in the campaign (approximately 800 kilometers)
21–22 September 1939	Return march to Brest-Litowsk and German-Soviet field parade
23 September to 1 October 1939	Billeting of the division in East Prussia
5 October to 29 November 1939	The regiment returns to its peacetime garrisons in Wünsdorf (*Oberst Freiherr* von Funck assumes command of the regiment on 15 October)
29 November 1939 to February 1940	The forces of the division move to the Osnabrück-Warendorf area.
February to April 1940	The division crosses the Rhine and occupies assembly areas in its operations area along the Western Front
	Preparations for the attack in the West

Between the campaigns: Lieutenants in the regiment. From the left: *Leutnant* Steinbrecher, *Leutnant* Fricke (killed in action in Africa in 1942) and *Leutnant* Zorn.

September 1939: Tanks of the regiment cross the Bug.

2 September 1939: The tank regiment in the attack in the Graudenz area.

The regiment moves out. The vehicle in the foreground is a *Panzerbefehlswagen III*.

Attack on a farmstead defended by Poles.

The light tank platoon of the regimental headquarters during a break in operations. Note the Polish border marker one of the men is holding.

Mobile command post. The commander of the 2nd Battalion, *Major* von Wilcke, is sitting at the table.

5 September 1939: The Supreme Commander of the Armed Forces visits the *XIX. Armee-Korps (mot). Generalmajor* Rommel, who was the commander of Hitler's security detail at the time, is seen with the map in the crook of his left arm.

Adolf Hitler among the soldiers.

A *Panzer IV* of the 4th
Company crosses a
body of water.

A wheeled vehicle (Kfz. 4) of the regiment with a twin machine gun for antiaircraft defense.

A *Panzer I* in an assembly area. Note the field vegetation and the improvised quarters.

Commanders in
conference with Guderian:
Oberstleutnant Conze is
to the viewer's far left
and *Oberst* Stumpff, the
commander of the *3. Panzer-
Brigade*, is wearing the full
Panzer uniform.

The regiment deployed for the attack.

A *Panzer II* of the regimental headquarters in a Polish village.

A burned-out *Panzer IV* of the 8th Company.

Gravesite for the crew of *824*, a *Panzer IV.*

Panzerschütze Arnold
Grassnick of the 5th
Company, who was
killed in action on 18
September.

A *Panzer I* of the company bears his name, a custom that was frequently followed in the early war years.

On the way home.

The harbor at Pillau at the beginning of October 1939. The regiment's tracked vehicles are loaded on to transport ships.

5 November 1939: The regimental band holds a concert for the wounded from the campaign in Poland. The text reads: "Sunday, 5 November, 1600 hours (4 o'clock). Charitable concert for the benefit of the wounded of the tank regiment in Poland at the Flower Gardens in Oberschöneweide. Performing: The music corps and choir of *Panzer-Regiment 5*. Directing: *Stabsmusikmeister* Taege. The entrance cost of 50 *Pfennige* will be given exclusively to the wounded. The rapid end of the war in Poland is especially thanks to the advancing armored forces, in addition to the magnificent performance of the *Luftwaffe* and other forces. Those who remained at home can especially thank the wounded by attending the charitable event in large numbers."

Winter 1939–1940: Soldiers of the regiment in a garrison in Hamm.

Spring 1940: The regiment moves by rail to the western frontier, with the local populace offering support.

CHAPTER 4

Panzer-Regiment 5 in the Campaign in the West, 1940

1. Organization and Strength of the Regiment for the Campaign

By the beginning of January 1940, the regiment had been brought up to its TO&E authorized strengths of 1 March 1939 in tanks as the result of new issues and repairs. For the start of the campaign in the West on 10 May 1940, there are no data available concerning the actual on-hand strength for the

Type of Tank	On hand strength of *Panzer-Regiment 5* at 10 May 1940 (estimate)	Authorized strength of the regiment (minus the 3rd and 7th companies), in accordance with TO&E dated 1 March 1939
klPzBefWg	} 13	9
PzBefWg III		4
Panzerkampfwagen I	49	54
Panzerkampfwagen II	60	65
Panzerkampfwagen III	20	10
Panzerkampfwagen IV	12	12
Summe	154	154

regiment, although there are data available for the *3. Panzer-Brigade.*[1]

Therefore, the following should be considered only as an approximation of the strength of the regiment on 10 May:

1. Author's Note: Jentz, *Die deutsche Panzertruppe*, Vol. I, 120.

According to this, a number of *Panzer III's* were issued from the beginning of the year to the beginning of May, even if only in modest numbers. This is as a consequence of a special TO&E dated 21 February 1940 (below) that was designed for light tank companies.[2]

2. Author's Note: Jentz, 107.

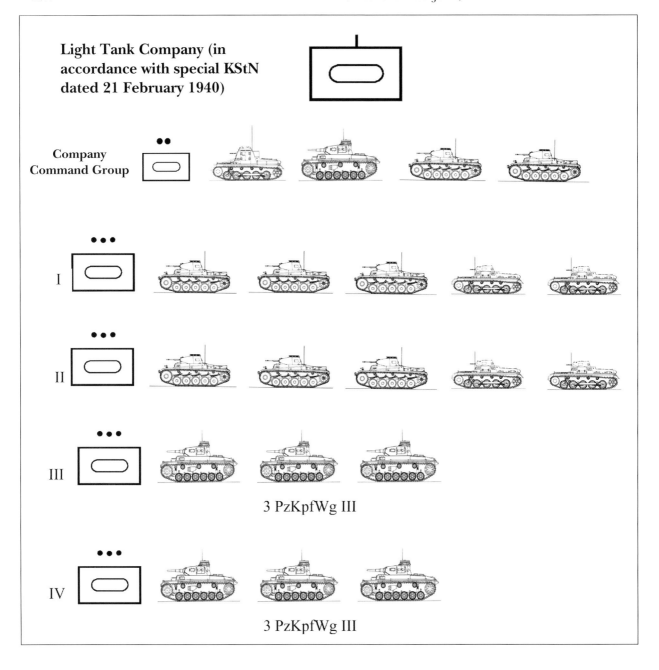

Light Tank Company (in accordance with special KStN dated 21 February 1940)

Company Command Group

I

II

III

3 PzKpfWg III

IV

3 PzKpfWg III

Despite that, the tank regiments of the *3. Panzer-Division*, as well as those of the *4. Panzer-Division* (*Panzer-Regiment 35* and *Panzer-Regiment 36*) were still primarily equipped with *Panzer I's* and *Panzer II's*. The other armor divisions had a large proportion of *Panzer III's* and *Panzer IV's.*[3]

The regiment was still under the command of *Oberst Freiherr* von Funck at the start of the campaign. The 1st Battalion had its 1st, 2nd and 4th Companies, while the 2nd Battalion retained the 5th, 6th and 8th Companies. The regiment also had its organic maintenance company. The *Panzer-Lehr-Abteilung* was no longer attached to the regiment, having been sent to the *9. Panzer-Division* instead.

In accordance with orders issued on 26 October 1939, the large white crosses disappeared as national identity markers and were replaced by black *Balkenkreuze* ("beam crosses") with white outlines. They were placed on the hull sides and rear.[4]

Based on the experiences of the campaign in Poland, the early-model *Panzer III's*—A to D—were upgraded to the model E and F variants from February to April. The primary feature of the upgrade was the bolting on of 2-centimeter armor plates to the hull and turret front.[5] The armor on the *Panzer II* was also reinforced with 2-centimeter plating on the hull and turret front.

The divisions were identifiable by markers that were placed on the vehicles. For the armor divisions, the newly designed insignia were painted in yellow. It is believed the design for the *3. Panzer-Division* was loosely based on the *Brandenburger Tor* for the Berlin-based division. The insignia is illustrated below.

---

3. Translator's Note: There were also large numbers of Czech tanks built by Skoda that were pressed into German service, the most prominent of which was the *Panzer 38(t)*, which was actually superior to both the *Panzer I* and the *Panzer II.*

---

4. Author's Note: Jentz, 105.

5. Author's Note: Jentz, 109.

The regiment proper did not have its own insignia, using instead the divisional one. A *Panzer IV* of the regiment during the campaign in the West. The divisional insignia can plainly be seen next to the *Balkenkreuz.*

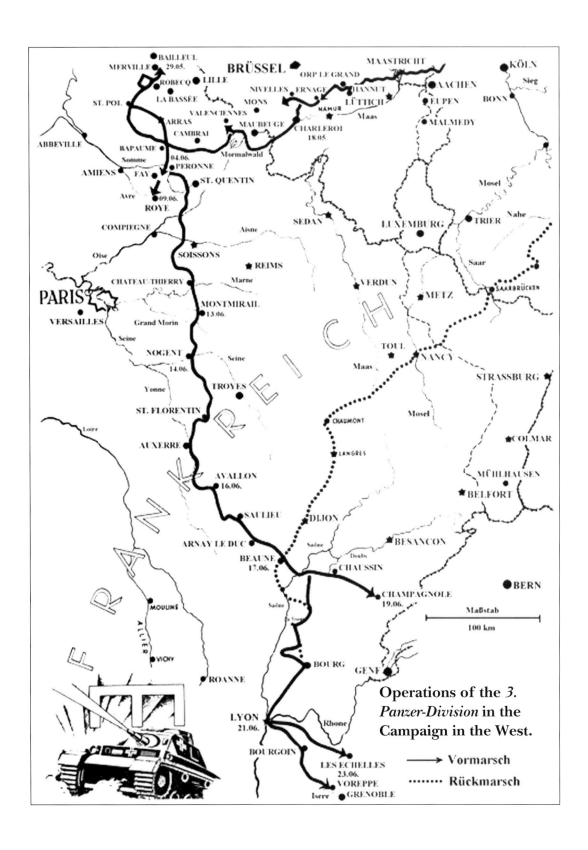

Operations of the *3. Panzer-Division* in the Campaign in the West.

→ Vormarsch

⋯⋯ Rückmarsch

2. Conduct of Operations from 10 May to 25 June 1940

German forces crossed the borders of Luxembourg, Holland, Belgium and France on the morning of 10 May 1940 in accordance with "Case Yellow," the operations order. *Heeresgruppe B*, under the command of *Generaloberst* von Bock, was employed on the right wing. It had three armor divisions reporting to it. The *3. Panzer-Division*, along with the *29. Infanterie-Division (mot)* and the *4. Panzer-Division* were part of the *XVI. Armee-Korps (mot)* of *General der Kavallerie* Hoepner, which initially was allocated to the *6. Armee* of *Generaloberst* von Reichenau. The *3. Panzer-Division* was directed to advance as rapidly as possible across the Meuse River and west of Maastricht to the Albert Canal, opening the way for the *6. Armee* to continue the advance in the direction of Brussels. The division was reinforced by *MG-Bataillon 7*, the *II./Flak-Lehr-Regiment* and the *II./Artillerie-Regiment 49*.[6]

The approach march of the division started around 1000 hours on 10 May. The division initially moved in two march groups from the area around Krefeld to the southwest in the direction of Aachen. This time, in contrast to the campaign in Poland, the division was not in the first wave. It followed the *4. Panzer-Division. Oberst* Kühn, the commander of the *3. Panzer-Brigade*, was in command of one of the march groups, which marched in the following sequence: *Panzerjäger-Abteilung 39*, divisional headquarters, *Nachrichten-Abteilung 39*, headquarters of the *3. Panzer-Brigade*, *Panzer-Regiment 6*, *Panzer-regiment 5*, the *3./Panzer-Pionier-Bataillon 39*, one battery of the *II./Flak-Lehr-regiment* and one and one half fuel columns. The forces spent the night in assembly areas and billets along the Erkelenz-Linnich road.

On 11 May, the march continued in the direction of the German-Dutch border. The blown-up bridges

over the Meuse continued to cause traffic stoppages, since the formations employed up front could not be funneled across the provisional bridges very quickly. The lead elements of the division reached the Dutch border around 1500 hours on 11 May. The lead columns moved through Maastricht late in the afternoon and crossed the Meuse on a pontoon bridge. During the night of 11–12 May, the first elements of the division reached the Albert Canal and entered Belgium.

On 12 May, the lead elements made their first enemy contact and were located outside of Hannut by evening. The French forces, for their part, had also advanced into Belgium in an effort to interdict the German attack. Facing the *XVI. Armee-Korps (mot)* were 90 Somua and 140 Hotchkiss tanks.[7]

On 13 May 1940, the first large-scale tank engagement of World War II started. The divisions from the capitals of Germany and France faced each other—the *3. Panzer-Division* of Berlin and the 3rd Mechanized Division of Paris. The *3. Panzer-Brigade* moved into its attack positions around 1230 hours, while *Ju 87's*—the feared *Stuka*—attacked identified enemy positions. *Panzer-Regiment 5* was reinforced by elements of the divisional antitank battalion. The brigade moved out and won the high ground along the Gette River around 1300 hours. *Panzer-Regiment 5* eliminated an enemy antitank-gun belt and crossed the Gette around 1430 hours on a provisional bridge. The brigade was attacked in the left flank by French tanks from the south and in the right flank from the northwest in the vicinity of Orp le Grand. The *Panzer I's* and *II's* were held back, while the *Panzer III's* and *IV's* took up the firefight with the enemy. The German tanks were employed doctrinally, that is, as platoons and companies and formed kill zones capable of firing quickly. By contrast, the French tanks were employed piecemeal and became involved in individual engagements. Consequently, they were knocked out or forced to pull back. By 1600 hours, the fighting had been decided, and the two tank

6. Author's Note: *Geschichte der 3. Panzer-Division*, 41. Translator's Note: The machine-gun battalion eventually became *Kradschützen-Bataillon 64* of the *14. Panzer-Division*. The heavy artillery battalion eventually became the 3rd Battalion of *Artillerie-Regiment 75*, the divisional artillery.

7. Author's Note: Jentz, 117.

Destroyed bridge over the Meuse near Maastricht (Holland).

13 May 1940: Knocked-out Somua after the tank engagement at Hannut. The soldier on the left wears the insignia on his right sleeve indicating he is a standard bearer for the battalion (in this case, the 2nd Battalion). Normally, this insignia was not worn in the field.

A knocked-out *Panzer II* of the regiment after the engagement at Hannut on 13 May. The supplemental armor around the driver's compartment and on the front side of the turret can be seen to good advantage. The divisional insignia is also visible on the side of the hull above the antenna stowage rail.

regiments could continue the attack west, effectively supported by the fires of *Artillerie-Regiment 75* and the *II./Artillerie-Regiment 49.*

The regiment advanced past Orp le Grand to the south and pursued the withdrawing 3rd Mechanized Division into the night of 13–14 May. The French had lost some 30 Somua and 70 Hotchkiss tanks that day. The *6. Armee* intended to continue the attack in the direction of Nivelles.

Around 0900 hours on 14 May, the *3. Panzer-Division* moved out again, with the *3. Panzer-brigade* in the lead. The French initially conducted a delaying action, with the result that the attack made good progress. As the attack spearheads neared the French Dyle Position (named after the river) in the Ernage area, the resistance began to stiffen. The commanding general of the *XVI. Armee-Korps*

(mot), General Hoepner, ordered an attack at 0900 hours on 15 May with both the *3. Panzer-Division* and the *4. Panzer-Division* on line to break through the Dyle Position on both sides of Ernage.[8] The *3. Panzer-Division* was facing elements of three French divisions (3rd Mechanized, 1st Moroccan and 1st Infantry) and elements of two Belgian divisions (2nd and 7th Infantry).

By the evening of 15 May, the *3. Panzer-Brigade*, together with the *3. Schützen-Brigade*, was able to penetrate the French positions west of Ernage, albeit with heavy losses. On 16 May, the attack was continued, transitioning to a pursuit of the defeated enemy.

At 0100 hours on 17 May, the division formed an advance guard, spearheaded by the reconnaissance

---

8. Author's Note: *Geschichte der 3. Panzer-Division*, 41.

battalion, to take the crossings over the Canel-de-Bruxelles which ran north-south west of Nivelles. The rest of the division followed in three march groups. After the crossings were forced, the division advanced southwest in the direction of Charleroi. This was followed by a short break in offensive operations, while the division was switched to the *4. Armee* of *Generaloberst* von Kluge.

On the morning of 20 May, the lead elements of the division crossed the French border in the vicinity of Maubeuge. The advance guard made first contact with the enemy around 1140 hours at the northeast corner of the Mormal Woods. The division was given the mission to go around the woods to the north so as to screen the northern flank of the *XVI. Armee-Korps (mot)* in the Valenciennes area. To accomplish that, a line of enemy bunkers on the northwestern edge of the Mormal Woods had to be taken first.

The regiment, together with *Panzer-Regiment 6*, started its attack around 0630 hours on 21 May, reinforced by motorized riflemen, artillery, *Flak*, engineers and antitank elements. It succeeded in breaking through the line of bunkers by that evening and advancing to the area south of Valenciennes.

On 22 May, the corps was pulled out of the line in that sector and then continued its attack to the southwest in the direction of Cambrai. The division's former sector was assumed by the *Leibstandarte SS Adolf Hitler*, Hitler's elite bodyguard formation that was roughly the size of a regiment. Marching at night, the *3. Panzer-Division* covered nearly 60 kilometers without enemy contact and reached the area east of Bapaume.

At 0900 on 23 May, the division received the mission from the corps to take bridges over the La Bassée Canal at Robecq as a prerequisite for the

This line of bunkers at the northwest corner of the Mormal Woods was broken by the regiment on 21 May.

breakthrough of the corps to the English Channel.[9] The forced crossing was completed by 26 May in the face of tough resistance from British forces. On 26 May, the division was temporarily attached to the *XXXXI. Armee-Korps (mot)* of *Generalleutnant* Reinhardt. Reinhardt's corps ordered the division to conduct an attack across the Lys Canal in the direction of Merville-Bailleul on 27 May.[10] The attack was launched at 0800 hours, with dismounted motorized riflemen leading the way and following a short artillery preparation. After a bridgehead across the canal had been established, the *3. Panzer-Brigade* was brought forward to take the hotly contested Merville. For the fighting, the 2nd Battalion of *Panzer-Regiment 6* was attached to the regiment.

The attack did not initially succeed and was called off that night. It was continued the next day under stormy and rainy weather. Merville fell in the course of the day. That evening, 28 May, the division was attached back to the *XVI. Armee-Korps (mot).*

Around 1100 hours on 29 May, with the motorized rifle brigade reinforced by tanks in the lead, the division continued its attack. In the area around Bailleul, the lead elements had to be held up, however, since the *6. Armee* was already advancing north to the east of them. By the evening of 29 May, the forward outposts of the *3. Panzer-Division* were 6 kilometers south of the French-Belgian border and 15 kilometers outside of Ypern, the bitterly contested battlefield of the First World War.

The forces of the division began occupying rest position during the night of 30 May–1 June in the area west of the La Bassée Canal. The regiment used the time primarily to maintain and repair tanks and materiel. On 1 June, orders were received to move the division to the Somme. The march started at 2100 hours on 2 June and proceeded via St. Pol, Arras and Bapaume to the south. The *3. Panzer-Brigade*

9. Author's Note: *Geschichte der 3. Panzer-Division*, 59.
10. Author's Note: *Geschichte der 3. Panzer-Division*, 61.

occupied assembly areas in the Peronne area. This signaled the end of the first phase of the Campaign in the West.

✠

On 4 June, *Oberst* Kühn, the commander of the *3. Panzer-Brigade*, wrote the following after-action report:

I. Tank-versus-tank combat

The brigade was able to hold its own in numerous engagements against enemy tanks, including the major engagement on 13 May against the French 3rd Mechanized Division.

In all, 87 "kills" have been confirmed. The brigade encountered French R 35's, D 2's, Hotchkiss's and Somua's and British carriers and Carden Lloyd 1938's. There was no contact with the French B 2.

A. Effectiveness of friendly weapons against enemy armor

The only effective German weapon against French tanks is the 7.5-centimeter tank main gun with its antitank round. The 3.7-centimeter antitank round is ineffective against the Somua and the D 2 at normal combat ranges. In general, the 3.7-centimeter antitank round penetrates at ranges less than 300 meters, if the round strikes horizontally. The 3.7-centimeter antitank round has not met expectations and is considered inadequate in combat operations against modern enemy armor.

Direct hits with the 7.5-centimeter high-explosive round at distances between 600 and 800 meters showed no effect against the Somua with either impact or delayed fuses.

The 2-centimeter antitank round was in-effective against all French tanks in terms of penetrating ability and had only a moral effect.

Both of the British vehicles, on the other hand, were penetrated by the 2-centimeter round at all combat distances.

The considerable consumption of ammunition in combating enemy armor can be traced back to the insufficient ability to penetrate with the 2- and 3.7-centimeter ammunition. For example, during the major engagement on 13 May, nearly 100 percent of the 7.5- and 3.7-centimeter rounds were fired. The brigade had to take on more ammunition before it could continue the attack.

The outfitting of German turrets in terms of traversing mechanisms, weapons cradles and sighting devices was completely successful. It is vastly superior to that of the French. That made it possible for the Germans to enjoy superior firepower.

B. The effectiveness of enemy weapons against friendly tanks

The effectiveness of enemy weapons against our tanks was negligible due to the targeting and aiming devices of the French tanks. In contrast, the effectiveness of the French 4.7-centimeter antitank gun was very good. That cannon penetrated all German armor at every location up to a distance of 600 meters.

The short 3.7-centimeter antitank gun was worthless. The French turret arrangements were primitive compared to the German ones. The main gun could not fire on the move and had only a limited rate of fire while stationary. Aiming at moving targets is more difficult than in German tanks.

C. Tactical lessons

The tank-versus-tank engagement was conducted by the *Panzer II's*, *III's* and *IV's*. The *Panzer IV* bore the main burden, since it was only hits from its antitank rounds that penetrated with certainty. The *Panzer III* had to close to short range for its 3.7-centimeter main gun to penetrate.

Although the 2-centimeter main gun never succeeded in penetrating the armor of a French tank, hits from the bursting rounds of the 2-centimeter main gun frequently led to the enemy crews waving a white flag or bailing out and giving up the fight.

In general, engagements were conducted from a stationary position during a firing halt. The unbelievably bad capability of the French tanks to aim and hit targets, made it possible for our tanks to approach closely in a zigzag maneuver to good firing range and thus carry the attack forward.

The French tank crews had bad fighting morale. In contrast to the German tanks, they never sought out tank-versus-tank engagements. The German tank crews possessed a feeling of absolute superiority against the French armored forces.

II. Tanks versus antitank guns

A. Effectiveness of enemy antitank guns against friendly tanks

The aiming accuracy of the antitank guns: The French 4.7-centimeter antitank gun is good; the French 2.5-centimeter antitank gun is very good and the British 4-centimeter antitank gun is terrific.

Penetrating capability of enemy antitank guns against all German tanks at a good strike angle: The French 4.7-centimeter antitank gun is very good up to a distance of 600 meters; the French 2.5-centimeter antitank gun is very good up to a distance of 400 meters. (The frontal armor of a *Panzer III* was cleanly penetrated by a 2.5-centimeter antitank gun. Tests conducted against captured tanks have shown that the 2.5-centimeter antitank gun is superior to the 3.7-centimeter German gun.)

The British 4-centimeter antitank gun is terrific (better and more effective than the

Oberst Kühn, seen here as a general officer, was the commander of the *3. Panzer-Brigade* during the campaign in the West. For the breakthrough of the Weygand Line, he was awarded the Knight's Cross to the Iron Cross on 4 July.

French 4.7-centimeter antitank gun) up to a distance of 800 meters. The British antitank rifle can most likely only penetrate a *Panzer I* or *Panzer II* at close range (little experience).

B. The effectiveness of tanks against antitank guns

By far, the most effective weapon against antitank guns is the 7.5-centimeter main gun with high-explosive rounds.

The 2-centimeter main gun has shown itself to be particularly effective against antitank guns. The magazines were loaded in a 1-to-1 ratio of armor-piercing to high-explosive rounds. Smoke rounds were not used.

III. Tanks against motorized infantry

In operations against motorized infantry, tanks have proven their absolute superiority. As long as [the enemy] had no antitank guns available, the enemy infantry was shot to pieces by them.

The drum magazine and the fixed mount of the *MG 34* caused constant stoppages—an unsuitable weapon of war.

IV. Armored engagements in special situations

Tanks are not suited for fighting in built-up areas or woods. The street fighting in the city of Merville demonstrated clearly that antitank guns emplaced in rooms behind windows on ground level cannot be localized. Tanks did not have a chance against weapons employed in that manner in street fighting.

The 7.5-centimeter high-explosive round was the most effective in defeating the enemy in built-up areas. The machine guns and 2-centimeter main guns were practically worthless. It appears that a flamethrower tank is necessary for combating pockets of resistance in basements and houses.

V. Recommendations

The following is based on the previously cited lessons learned:

A. Weapons

The mounting of a more effective weapon (4.7-centimeter or 5-centimeter) in the *Panzer III* in place of the 3.7-centimeter main gun is urgently needed. In comparison to the remaining requests, this one has the highest priority and urgency.

Due to its constant stoppages, the *MG 34* in its current form with drum magazines and fixed mount is unusable for combat. A solution is necessary.

The outfitting of the *Panzer IV* with three machine guns (as in the *Panzer III*) is desirable. The mounting of a rangefinder in the *Panzer IV* is likewise desirable.

The mounting of a machine gun or a submachine gun in a ball mount for close-in defense oriented to the rear is desirable.

The large command and control armored vehicle in its current form—without effective weapons—cannot be tolerated. It was been shown that the vehicle needs a main gun for self defense in tank engagements, as well as when it encounters antitank guns. It is recommended that a *Panzer III* be converted to a command and control armored vehicle by the installation of [additional] radio sets. The extendable antenna mast can be mounted outside the tank instead of on the inside.

B. Armor

The armor protection on the *Panzer III* and especially the *Panzer IV* is insufficient. The *Panzer III* was penetrated on the front slope by the terrific French 2.5-centimeter antitank gun. That gun is difficult to make out due to the lack of a muzzle flash.

The additional armor on the *Panzer II* proved effective. The main gun mantlet was penetrated several times; reinforcement is necessary.

C. Speed

The speed of the German tanks proved to be extremely effective. In the future, emphasis should be placed on maintaining a minimum speed of 30 kilometers an hour in normal terrain. French tank crews and antitank gun crews taken prisoner reported that the main problem in hitting German tanks was their speed.

In summary, the tactical fundamentals for the employment of armored forces proved themselves.

The feeling of superiority on the part of our armored forces with regard to the enemy is primarily based in our better fighting morale and, secondly, in our superior ability to fire. The armor on the German tanks and the number of armored vehicles with [heavy] guns are worse or less than in the French armored forces. Improvements in that area are necessary.

During the course of the campaign, the Tank Assault Badge in Silver (*Panzerkampfabzeichen*) was awarded for the first time to crewmembers of the regiment. The award had been created on 20 December 1939 at the same time as the Infantry Assault Badge by the Commander-in-Chief of the Army, *Generaloberst* Brauchitsch. The award was regulated as follows:[11]

> The Tank Assault Badge in Silver can be awarded to officers, noncommissioned officers and enlisted personnel of tank units, who, effective 1 January 1940, have participated in a minimum of three separate engagements on three different days as a tank or armored command & control vehicle commander, armored crewman, armored driver or armored radio operator, whereby the tank crew had to participate actively in the fighting.
>
> The Tank Assault Badge is worn on the left breast…in and out of duty.

The badge was designed by the artist and illustrator, Wilhelm Ernst Peekhaus, in Berlin.

Up until September 1942, the division commander had approval authority. Following that date, the regimental commander was authorized to present the award. The regiment was responsible for maintaining a list of qualifying engagements. The company commanders then determined which soldiers met the conditions and assembled their names on lists. The request for the award was then forwarded with the company commander's signature, once the requisite number of days had been obtained. The awardee was given a certificate in addition to the badge.

11. Author's Note: Doehle, *Die Auszeichnungen des Groß-deutschen Reichs*, page 104.

The Tank Assault Badge in Silver

On 1 June 1940, the Commander-in-Chief of the Army instituted a similar award in bronze for members of the motorized rifle regiments—renamed *Panzergrenadiere* in the fall of 1942—the motorcycle infantry battalions and the armored reconnaissance formations of the divisions. The award conditions were the same as those of the badge in silver.

For the regiment, the second phase of the campaign in the West started on 5 June with the attack on the Weygand Line southwest of Peronne.

The attack started at 0530 hours after an artillery preparation consisting of 384 tubes and sorties by the *Luftwaffe*. Despite strong enemy artillery fire, the division's two tank regiments advanced as far as the Hallu area, some 30 kilometers southwest of Peronne, by 0900 hours. The motorized riflemen earmarked to follow were held up by the villages along the Weygand Line, which had been transformed into

Werner Trodler in 1943 wearing the black
Panzer uniform with the Tank Assault Badge
in Silver.

Award caption: Trodler's award certificate for
service in the 6th Company. The award was
presented during the campaign in North Africa
and signed by the division commander at the
time, *Generalmajor* von Radow.

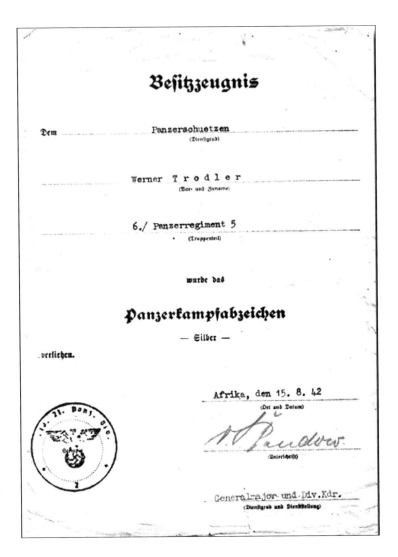

strongpoints. As a result, the *3. Panzer-Brigade* was all
by itself far in front of the division at noon. In the
attack, *Panzer-Regiment 6* had lost 30 tanks. During
the night of 5–6 June, the brigade had to fend off
strong enemy counterattacks in the Hallu area, with
no sign of the infantry. The tanks started to suffer
from a lack of fuel and ammunition.

On the morning of 6 June, the motorized
infantry succeeded in breaking through to the
tanks. That signified the decisive breakthrough of
the defensive position upon which the French had

pinned their hopes. The brigade commander would
later receive the Knight's Cross to the Iron Cross
for that operation. That afternoon, the *3. Panzer-Brigade* formed up under hot temperatures and
cloudless skies to pursue the enemy to the south
in the direction of the Avre, which was crossed that
evening, despite enemy air attacks.

The attack was successfully continued from 7 to 9
June as far as the Roye area. At that point, the division
was pulled out of the front lines and moved back to
Peronne. The troop elements of the division were

The Marne is crossed east of Chateau-Thierry on 12 June.

able to rest for two days there. The *XVI. Armee-Korps (mot)* then assembled in the St. Quentin–Soissons area on the right wing of the *9. Armee* of *General der Infanterie* Strauß.

In rainy weather, the spearhead of the division, the *3. Panzer-Brigade,* crossed the Marne east of Chateau-Thierry around 1400 hours on 12 June. Despite the onset of darkness, the attack made good progress forward.

On 13 June, the regiment succeeded in taking a bridge over the Grand Morin south of Montmirail intact. The tanks continued the assault in the direction of the Seine. The regiment formed the division's main effort for the thrust in the direction of Nogent. For that operation, the 2nd Battalion of *Schützen-Regiment 3* was attached to it.

The French strongpoint resistance was quickly broken. During the night of 13–14 June, the bridges over the seine at Nogent were taken by surprise by *Major Ritter Edler* von Peter's 2nd Battalion, along with supporting motorized riflemen and engineers. Nogent was captured and numerous prisoners taken.

The bridgehead was expanded until noon on 14 June and reconnaissance conducted towards the south. The corps was already far behind the French front. The German forces were ordered to pursue the French forces vigorously. *Kampfgruppe Kühn*, of which the regiment was a part, advanced past endlessly long columns of French refugees and against only weak enemy resistance into the evening of 14 June, reaching the St. Florentin area.

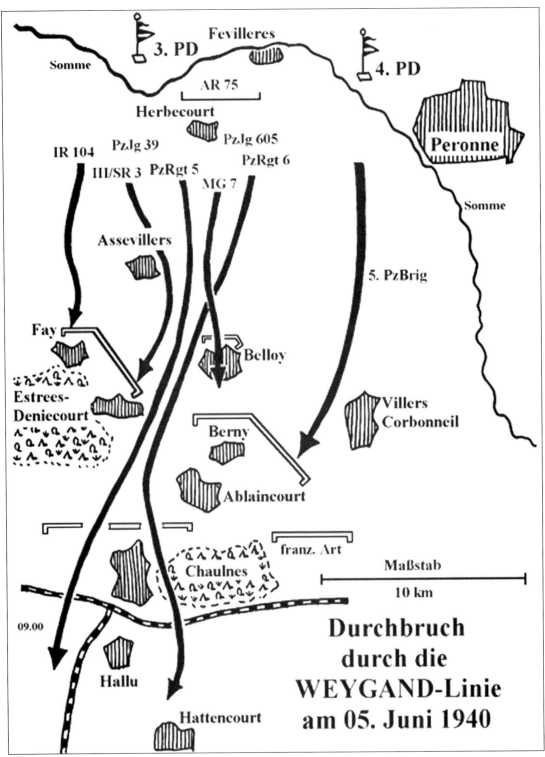

Breakthrough through the Weygand Line on 5 June 1940

The French Army increasingly showed signs of dissolution. During the night of 14–15 June, *Major* Hohmann's 1st Battalion reinforced *Schützen-Regiment 3* in the capture of St. Florentin. A fuel depot was captured with more than 6 million liters of fuel, and the constant fuel problems of the tankers were solved for a short while.

The division moved out around 1400 hours on 15 June to advance in the direction of Auxerre. Following the reconnaissance battalion, the *3. Panzer-Brigade* formed the vanguard of the division.

Moving through Auxerre, Avalon was reached early in the morning of 16 June without encountering appreciable enemy resistance. Because of the un-expectedly rapid advance, the tanks were forced to use commercial road maps in lieu of military maps. The French were surprised whenever the German tankers appeared.

By the afternoon of 16 June, the *3. Panzer-Brigade* was already outside of Saulieu. There it was hit in the left flank by Hotchkiss tanks. The enemy tanks belonged to those troop elements that had previously been positioned along the Maginot Line and which were then attempting to withdraw to the west. The enemy attack was turned back and the Saulieu taken. There was no longer any sign of unified command and control among the enemy forces.

Major Hohmann, the commander of the 1st Battalion. He is seen in the cupola of a *Panzer IV*, which has been christened the *Prinz Eugen*.

A *kleiner Panzerbefehlswagen* of the headquarters of the 1st Battalion. On the rear deck in a field-gray tunic is the future *Major* and Knight's Cross recipient Hans Sandrock.

The division then advanced along good improved roads straight through the fertile Burgundy region with its meadows, grain fields and vineyards. By the evening of 16 June, Arnay le Duc was taken, albeit only after casualty-intensive house-to-house fighting. Beaune was taken the next day, and the division was placed under the command and control of the *12. Armee* of *Generaloberst* List.

By noon on 18 June, a bridgehead over the Saône was established. From that point forward, the division no longer encountered any serious resistance. That same day, the Doubs near Chaussin was also crossed.

19 June was a day of rest and nice weather for the division. Once again, maintenance on the vehicles and equipment took precedence. Only the divisional reconnaissance battalion was employed, and it was able to advance as far as Champagnole without encountering any enemy resistance. That meant that the lead elements of the division were only 15 kilometers from the Swiss border that evening. After the French field army in Alsace had become encircled, the division was given a new avenue of advance: downstream along the Rhône.

The German Army High Command announced that the limit of forward advance for the ground forces was a line defined by Lyon in the east and Bordeaux in the west. The division, as part of the *XVI. Armee-Korps (mot)*, followed the *XIV. Armee-Korps (mot)* in the direction of Lyon on 20 June. The enemy was no longer capable of offering any substantive resistance.

The lead elements of the regiment outside of Lyon on 20 June.

On 21 June, the division reached Lyon and took up billets in numerous small villages around the city in the days that followed. The purchase of fruit and everyday items was a welcome change-of-pace for the soldiers.

The next mission for the division was to attack east in the direction of Grenoble to protect the left flank of the corps and, if possible, establish contact with the Italian forces. In the fortified area between the Mediterranean and Montblanc, there were still eight enemy divisions and three fortress brigades employed. Since most of those forces had not been involved in the fighting up to that point, it was believed they would offer stiff resistance. There was bleak and rainy weather on 23 June. The division moved out in the morning with a northern and

southern arm for the advance east. The regiment was part of the southern group under the command of *Oberst* Kühn. At the entry to Grenoble Valley, the battle group ran into abatis that were guarded by antitank guns. Even after the obstacles and guard force were eliminated, the continued march proved difficult because of the steep mountain roads. The French defended effectively from antitank-gun and machine-gun positions, supported by artillery and mortars. After arduously working its way forward, the southern battle group reached Voreppe by the afternoon.

The lead tanks of the regiment started to receive artillery fire as they approached the Isère Canal and were held up by obstacles in the road. *Oberst* Kühn ordered *Schützen-Regiment 3* to move forward, but its

A *Panzer III* of the *3. Panzer-Division* in Isère Valley in the foothills to the Alps.

attack stalled in the face of casualties taken under heavy enemy fire. The division ordered the attack to be temporarily cancelled at 1900 hours.

On 24 June, Kühn forces also made no progress. The fires being received from the area in front of the Grenoble fortress prevented the division from entering the French West Alps. The northern battle group of the division was able to advance as far as Les Echelles in heavy rain, however. On the evening of 24 June, the division called off all further attacks since it was expected that a ceasefire was to be announced shortly, and it wanted to avoid unnecessary losses. A message was received from the corps a short while later that the ceasefire would go into effect at 0125 hours on 25 June.[12]

The division initially remained in its forward positions, with outposts maintaining contact with the enemy. The last dead of the division were laid to rest, signaling the end of the campaign in the West.

The division, the brigade and the regiment had been in the thick of things from the very beginning, had participated in all of the decisive fighting, had made considerable sacrifices and had achieved noteworthy success. The division covered some 4,950 kilometers in fighting and marching its way across the Low Countries and France.[13] The prerequisites for that success were due in no small measures to the logistics forces as well, who performed their duties in a quiet and modest fashion, but conscientiously and loyally. They tirelessly brought fuel and ammunition forward, repaired disabled vehicles as quickly as possible and took care of the wounded.

On 29 June, the division received orders to start its march back to Germany on 1 July.

12. Author's Note: *Geschichte der 3. Panzer-Division*, 94.

13. Author's Note: *Geschichte der 3. Panzer-Division*, 95.

The tracked elements of the regiment are rail loaded for home. Here: vehicles of the 8th Company.

July 1940 in the *General-Lutz-Kaserne* in Wünsdorf. A view from a window in the billets of the 5th Company, with the 2nd Battalion's Fighting Vehicle Memorial in the foreground.

The movement started around 0700 hours on the designated day. The tracked elements were loaded on trains, while the wheeled elements road-marched. The route led through Lyon, Bourg, Beaune, Dijon, Langres and Chaumont to the borders of the *Reich*, which was crossed by the brigade on 5 July.

On 7 July, the division marched from Saarbrücken through Kaiserslautern and then on to Mainz, where a parade was conducted for the division commanders and high military dignitaries.[14]

14. Author's Note: *Geschichte der 3. Panzer-Division*, 98.

The tracked vehicles were loaded the same day and reached their peacetime garrisons over the next two days. The local populace greeted the troops enthusiastically and showered the soldiers with flowers, baked goods, drinks and cigarettes.

The units and formations conducted yet another pass-in-review for their commanders before maintenance and recovery for vehicles, weapons and equipment topped the list of priorities.

Oberst Freiherr von Funck, shown here as a general officer, led the regiment during the campaign in the West.

He was born in Aachen on 23 December 1891, took part in the Great War and then served in the *Reichswehr.* Promoted to *Oberst* on 1 December 1938, he was the military attaché in Lisbon starting on 1 January 1939. On 15 October 1935, he assumed command of the regiment.

On 13 October 1940, he succeeded *Oberst* Kühn in command of the *3. Panzer-Brigade.* Promoted to *Generalmajor,* he assumed command of the *7. Panzer-Division* on 15 February 1941. It was in that capacity that he was awarded the Knight's Cross to the Iron Cross on 15 July 1941 and the Oak Leaves to the Knight's Cross on 22 August 1943.

On 1 March 1944, he was promoted to *General der Panzertruppen,* assuming command of the *XXXXVII. Panzer-Korps* on 5 march of the same year.

He passed away in Viersen on 14 February 1979.

13. Lessons Learned

The winter of 1939–1940 and the following spring were used by the *Panzertruppe* to translate the lessons learned from the campaign in Poland into reality, at least as far as training was concerned. By contrast, the weapons had not changed much from 1939, since the time was much too short for that. Among the German leadership, the maxims of Guderian had been taken to heart: "Smash, don't slap!" and "A ticket to the final destination!" The operational idea for the campaign in the West came from the Chief-of-Staff of *Heeresgruppe A, Generalleutnant* von Manstein.[15] The operations plan called for a breakthrough by fast armored forces across apparently tank-proof terrain all the way to the English Channel, so as to cut the Allied armies in two and then destroy them piecemeal. Close cooperation between the *Panzertruppe* and the other branches was necessary, as was demonstrated in the organization of the armor divisions. Although the French and the English were numerically superior in France, their equipment,

organization, training and doctrinal principles were not. It was especially the French who saw the tanks as primarily just a support weapon for the infantry.

After the first phase of the campaign plan had turned out in favor of the Germans, the decisive battle for France was initiated with two armored groups attacking south. The armored wedge brought with it renewed success. Once again, a military victory was achieved in a short time—just six weeks—that has few equivalents in the history of warfare.

Decisively participating in that success were the 10 armored divisions. Approximately 2,500 German tanks, some of which were inferior to their English and French counterparts, had achieved success over 4,800 of their opponents by means of better leadership, tactics, combined-arms employment and training. The first large-scale tank engagements of the war demonstrated as their most pressing need the mounting of more effective weapons in the German tanks. In addition, reinforcement of the armor plating was also urgently needed.

15. Author's Note: Nehring, 128.

4. Overview

9 May 1940	Alert of the division in the Krefeld area
10 May 1940	The division marches as part of the *6. Armee* in two march groups to the German/Dutch border
11 May 1940	Crossing of the Albert canal west of Maastricht
12–13 May 1940	Tanks engagement in the Hannut area and along the Gette
14–16 May 1940	Breaking through the Dyle Position at Ernage
17–18 May 1940	Pursuit from the Dyle as far as the area around Nivelles and Charleroi
18 May 1940	Reorganization and allocation to the *4. Armee*
20–22 May 1940	Fighting for the Mormal Woods; breaking through the bunker positions north of the Mormal Woods
23–26 May 1940	Battle of Flanders; fighting on the La Bassée Canal at Robecq
27–29 May 1940	Fighting along the Lys Canal at Merville and to the north at Bailleul
5–6 June 1940	Breaking through the Weygand Line southwest of Peronne as part of the *6. Armee*
7–9 June 1940	Fighting along the Avre on both sides of Roye
12–13 June 1940	Fighting for the Marne and pursuit through Montmirail as far as the Seine at Nogent as part of the *9. Armee*
14–17 June 1940	Pursuit from the Seine as far as Côte d'Or; taking of St. Florentin, Auxerre, Avallon, Saulieu, Arney le Duc and Beaune
18–24 June 1940	Crossing of the Saône and Doubs; offensive operations as part of the *12. Armee* as far as the Isère in the Grenoble sector, at Les Echelles and Voreppe
25 June 1940	0135 hours: Ceasefire
1–9 July 1940	Return to peacetime garrisons

A common grave for some of the last to fall in the campaign in the West: *Leutnant* Schwandt (Headquarters of the 2nd Battalion), *Gefreiter* Irrgang (8th Company) and *Obergefreiter* Schlatholt (Headquarters of the 2nd Battalion). The average age of those killed in France was 23. This gravesite was erected on 23 June 1940 at Voreppe, near Grenoble.

Beginning of May 1940: The regiment forms up for moving out for the campaign in the West.

13 May 1940: The first major tank engagement of the Second World War is conducted on the high ground near Hannut.

A *Panzer II* of the regimental headquarters during a break in the action. The vehicle appears to have become "domesticated" for the campaign. Note also the fascines carried to facilitate the crossing of ditches and soft ground and the rifle slung across the gun mantlet. One of the crew prepares a snack.

Regimental headquarters tanks in the vicinity of Orp le Grand.

Pursuing the beaten enemy.

Situation briefing.

A *Panzer III* from a neighboring division has caught fire.

A dangerous opponent, the French *Char B*, armed with a 7.5-centimeter main gun in a limited-traverse sponson and a 4.7-centimeter main gun in a revolving turret. The most powerful and heavily armored tank on the battlefied at that time. The tank commander also served as the gunner, thus slowing down the ability of the vehicle to respond to the ever-changing battlefield.

A *Panzer II* of the light platoon of the regimental headquarters. *Gefreiter* Heinrich-Gustav Schlieper, on the viewer's right, wears the beret without the crash helmet, accounting for its small, squat appearance.

The regimental commander's command and control tank has to be recovered. The "G" on the front slope stands for Guderian, who had overall command of the armored forces the regiment was part of.

Oberleutnant Hans-Engelbert Modersohn. He was killed by an antitank-gun round on 27 May 1940, while serving as the adjutant of the 1st Battalion.

Oberleutnant Hans-Engelbert Modersohn's gravesite in May 1940 in France

Graves for the fallen of the regiment with field-expedient crosses. As was the German custom early in the war, the crosses bear the headgear of the fallen and, in this case, the jacket of one of the soldiers.

The advance in France. A *Panzer II* takes temporary cover.

A *Panzer I* of the 6th Company in a French village. *Leutnant* Hennig, seen on the viewer's right, has just been awarded the Iron Cross, Second Class, since the medal was only worn on the day of its award. He is also a recipient of the Tank Assault Badge in Silver.

Gefreiter Heinrich-Gustav Schlieper in front of a regimental *Panzer II.*

6 June 1940: The 2nd Company advances against the Weygand Line.

Crossing the Marne at Chateau-Thierry on 12 June. An 18-ton *FAMO* prime mover pulls a trailer across the provisional bridge.

The *R 02*, a *kleiner Panzerbefehlswagen I* of the regimental headquarters.

On 13 June 1940 *Oberfunkmeister* Fritz Heister, *Gefreiter* Werner Borgmann and *Gefreiter* Otto Hahn were killed in the *R 02*.

The gravesite for the crew of the *R 02*.

Preparing for operations.

A *Panzer II* of the 1st Company in a French village that has received a heavy artillery barrage or, more likely, a visit from the *Luftwaffe*.

Captured French tank factory in Auxerre. The vehicle hulls appear to be from Souma S 35s.

15 June: The attack south is continued. The tactical sign on the vehicle to the right is for a motorized infantry platoon, 8th Company.

The 5th Company in the attack.

A *Panzer III* of the regiment has landed in a tank trap and has to be recovered.

22 June: Tanks of the regiment in Bourgoin in the Lyon area.

Oberleutnant Hans Sandrock of the 1st Battalion Headquarters and his crew, several of whom have taken on distinctly Gallic features, wearing their berets French style and sporting goatees. The twin coaxial machine guns of the early-model *Panzer III* are seen to good advantage.

Return of the headquarters of the 1st Battalion and the regiment to the *Cambrai-Kaserne* on 9 July.

The 2nd Company has formed up in the *Cambrai-Kaserne*. Numerous soldiers have been awarded the Tank Assault Badge in Silver.

A *Panzer III* takes a run through a tank "bath" at the vehicle washing facilities at Wünsdorf.

R 00 leaves the "tub." Note the apparent "kill" marks on the commander's cupola, including an aircraft.

A *Panzer I* goes through the same procedure.

R 03 bears a plaque commemorating *Gefreiter* Otto Hahn, who was killed during the campaign in the West in *R 02*.

R 00 bears a plaque commemorating *Gefreiter* Werner Borgmann, who was killed in the same vehicle.

CHAPTER 5

Panzer-Regiment 5
prior to Employment in Africa

1. The Political Situation at the End of 1940 and Beginning of 1941

As it became apparent that the German Armed Forces were to emerge victorious from the campaign in the West, Italy, which was part of the Berlin-Rome "Axis," declared war on France on 11 June 1940. Italy's entry into the war did not result in the desired help for Germany. It soon became apparent that Italy was incapable of resolving any military issues without the assistance of Germany.

After Italian demands for French territory—Nice, Corsica, Tunis and parts of Algeria—were turned down by Hitler, Mussolini believed he would be able to be successful in North Africa on his own. On 13 September 1940, the Italian 10th Army of Marshall Graziani moved out from the Italian colony of Libya—a colony since 1912—in an offensive against the British in Egypt. The Italian soldiers were inadequately equipped with obsolete weapons; in addition, they were poorly led. They had fought for nearly three decades against natives in Libya and Abyssinia, but they had never fought against an army equipped with modern weaponry, such as the British had. After 80 kilometers, the Italians called off their attack at Sidi Barani, so as to firm up their logistical lines of communication.

On 6 December, the English 8th Army of General Archibald Wavell launched its counteroffensive. Advancing rapidly, it pushed the Italians back across the Egyptian-Libyan border and attacked the naval base at Tobruk, which was protected by Italian fortifications and took it on 22 January 1941. It was expected the British would continue their advance in the direction of Tripoli. Based on the critical development of the situation, Mussolini felt compelled to ask the Germans for military help.

✠

Although Hitler had declared on 9 January 1941 that he was "indifferent to the war in North Africa,"[1] he felt compelled to intervene. The following reasons tipped the scales, since the loss

- would have allowed England opportunities to intervene in French North Africa (Tunisia, Algeria and Morocco);
- would have allowed the blockade around Europe to be completed in the south;
- would have enabled the possibility of an invasion of Europe from the North African coastal region;
- would have tied down strong German forces on a southern front once an invasion was launched; and

1. Author's Note: Aberger, *Die 5. (lei.)/21. Panzer-Division in Nord Afrika, 1941–1943*, 20. Hereafter referred to as Aberger.

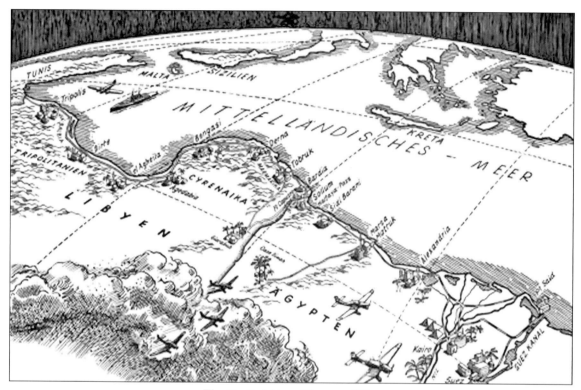

The North African Theater of War

- would lead to the loss of Italy as an ally.

All of these assumptions would later prove themselves correct in 1943.

Accordingly, Libya could not be permitted to be lost, either for political or military reasons.

The first support measure taken was the movement of the *X. Flieger-Korps*[2] with 200 aircraft to Sicily, from where it could strike British Mediterranean naval convoys and attack the British ground advance in North Africa.

2. Preparations for Employment in Africa

As early as 4 October 1940, in a discussion between Hitler and Mussolini, German assistance for an Italian offensive in north Africa had been arranged. On 11 October, the *3. Panzer-Division* was directed to be prepared to provide troop elements for employment in North Africa. The soldiers of the division were medically examined for fitness for duty in tropical climates; then preparations were put on hold for a while.[3]

In the face of the potential loss of Libya and the entreaties for help from Mussolini, the German Army High Command directed the formation of a "Holding Formation" for *Operation "Sonnenblume"* ("Sunflower") in accordance with *Führer* Directive No. 22. The

2. Translator's Note: X Air Corps.

3. Author's Note: *Die Geschichte der 3. Panzer-Division*, 98.

operation was intended to stabilize the Italian Front. The commander of the new formation was to be *Generalmajor Freiherr* von Funck, who had commanded the regiment in France.[4]

Von Funck flew to Libya to conduct a leader's reconnaissance. On 1 February 1941, he reported back to Hitler. It had been determined that a relatively weak "holding formation" would not be sufficient to help their pressured allies. Correspondingly, Hitler ordered the following:

- Expansion of the "holding formation" to a complete light division (*5. leichte Division*)
- Preparations for the sending of an armored division (*15. Panzer-Division*)

---

4. Author's Note: *Die Geschichte der 3. Panzer-Division*, 98.

- Command of the German Army forces in Libya by *Generalmajor* Rommel.[5]

Von Funck was released from his previous mission and assumed command of the *7. Panzer-Division* from Rommel. The *3. Panzer-Division* was directed to be the lead organization for providing forces for most of the units and formations composing the *5. leichte Division*. The division gave up *Panzer-Regiment 5*, commanded since 13 October 1940 by *Oberst* Olbrich, representing the largest formation it had to release.

The two battalions of the regiment prepared for their shipment to Africa. The regiment had received new *Panzer III's* with the 5-centimeter main gun and started to reorganize in accordance with a TO&E dated 1 February 1941.

---

5. Author's Note: Aberger, 22.

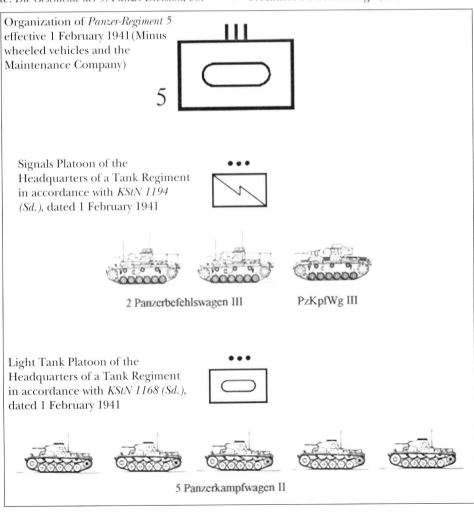

Organization of *Panzer-Regiment 5* effective 1 February 1941 (Minus wheeled vehicles and the Maintenance Company)

5

Signals Platoon of the Headquarters of a Tank Regiment in accordance with *KStN 1194 (Sd.)*, dated 1 February 1941

2 Panzerbefehlswagen III   PzKpfWg III

Light Tank Platoon of the Headquarters of a Tank Regiment in accordance with *KStN 1168 (Sd.)*, dated 1 February 1941

5 Panzerkampfwagen II

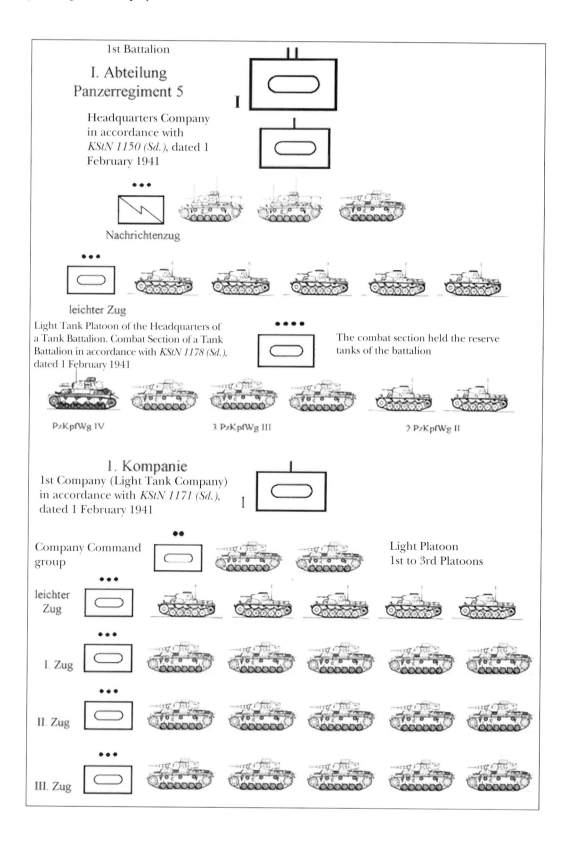

1st Battalion

I. Abteilung
Panzerregiment 5

I

Headquarters Company
in accordance with
KStN 1150 (Sd.), dated 1
February 1941

Nachrichtenzug

leichter Zug

Light Tank Platoon of the Headquarters of
a Tank Battalion. Combat Section of a Tank
Battalion in accordance with *KStN 1178 (Sd.)*,
dated 1 February 1941

The combat section held the reserve
tanks of the battalion

PzKpfWg IV   3 PzKpfWg III   2 PzKpfWg II

1. Kompanie

1st Company (Light Tank Company)
in accordance with *KStN 1171 (Sd.)*,
dated 1 February 1941

1

Company Command
group

Light Platoon
1st to 3rd Platoons

leichter
Zug

I. Zug

II. Zug

III. Zug

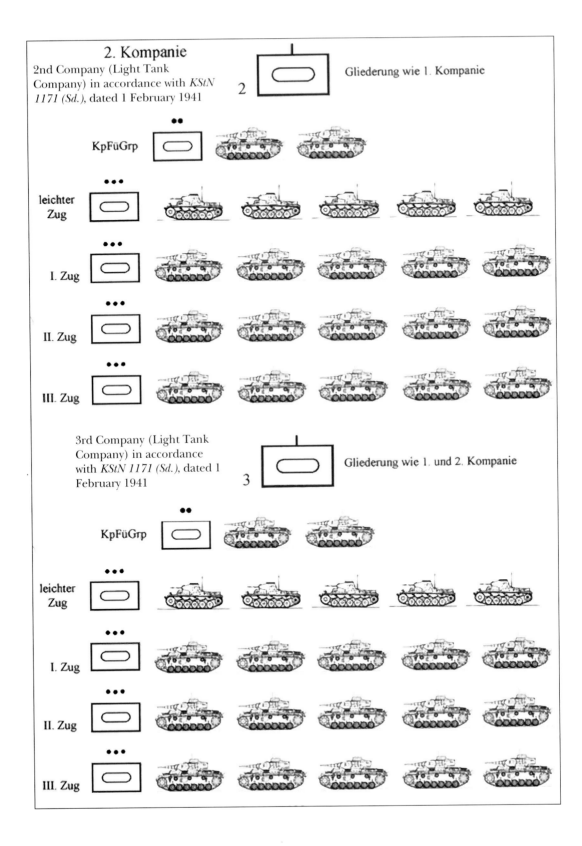

2. Kompanie

2nd Company (Light Tank Company) in accordance with *KStN 1171 (Sd.)*, dated 1 February 1941

2

Gliederung wie 1. Kompanie

KpFüGrp

leichter Zug

I. Zug

II. Zug

III. Zug

3rd Company (Light Tank Company) in accordance with *KStN 1171 (Sd.)*, dated 1 February 1941

3

Gliederung wie 1. und 2. Kompanie

KpFüGrp

leichter Zug

I. Zug

II. Zug

III. Zug

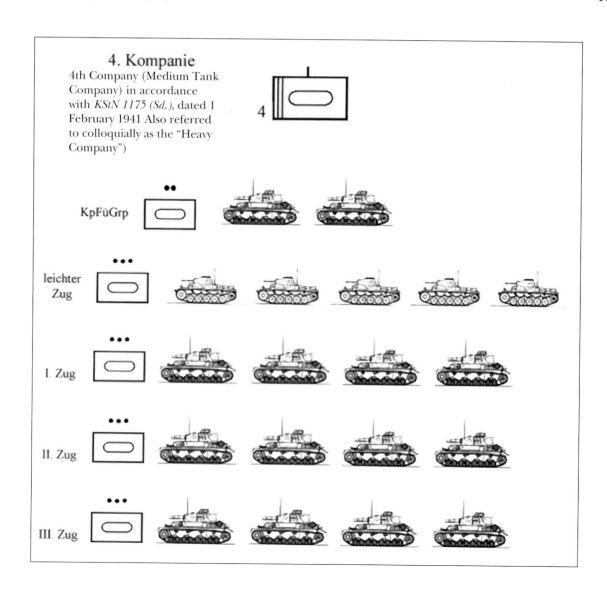

4. Kompanie

4th Company (Medium Tank Company) in accordance with *KStN 1175 (Sd.)*, dated 1 February 1941 Also referred to colloquially as the "Heavy Company")

KpFüGrp

leichter Zug

I. Zug

II. Zug

III. Zug

According to the TO&E (1 February 1941), a tank battalion was supposed to have the following tanks:

 2 *Panzerbefehlswagen III*

27 *Panzerkampfwagen II*

55 *Panzerkampfwagen III*

15 *Panzerkampfwagen IV*

99 tanks in each battalion

The entire regiment was allocated the following number of tanks:

  6 *Panzerbefehlswagen III*

59 *Panzerkampfwagen II*

111 *Panzerkampfwagen III*

 30 *Panzerkampfwagen IV*

206 tanks in each battalion

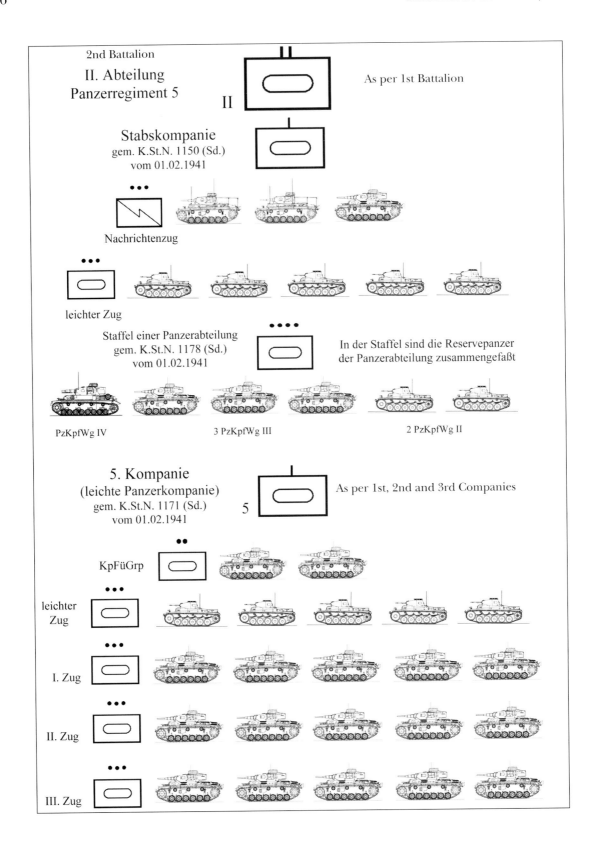

2nd Battalion

II. Abteilung
Panzerregiment 5   II

As per 1st Battalion

Stabskompanie
gem. K.St.N. 1150 (Sd.)
vom 01.02.1941

Nachrichtenzug

leichter Zug

Staffel einer Panzerabteilung
gem. K.St.N. 1178 (Sd.)
vom 01.02.1941

In der Staffel sind die Reservepanzer
der Panzerabteilung zusammengefaßt

PzKpfWg IV   3 PzKpfWg III   2 PzKpfWg II

5. Kompanie
(leichte Panzerkompanie)
gem. K.St.N. 1171 (Sd.)   5
vom 01.02.1941

As per 1st, 2nd and 3rd Companies

KpFüGrp

leichter
Zug

I. Zug

II. Zug

III. Zug

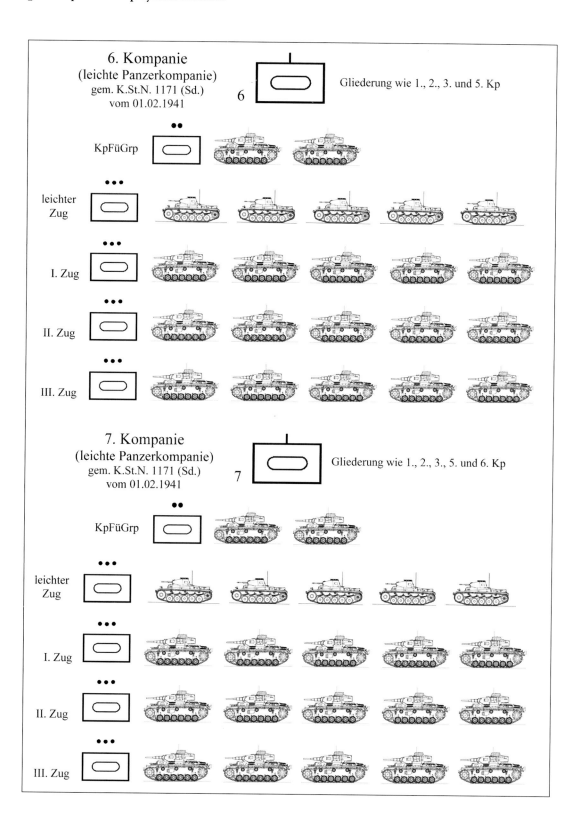

6. Kompanie
(leichte Panzerkompanie)
gem. K.St.N. 1171 (Sd.)
vom 01.02.1941

Gliederung wie 1., 2., 3. und 5. Kp

KpFüGrp

leichter Zug

I. Zug

II. Zug

III. Zug

7. Kompanie
(leichte Panzerkompanie)
gem. K.St.N. 1171 (Sd.)
vom 01.02.1941

Gliederung wie 1., 2., 3., 5. und 6. Kp

KpFüGrp

leichter Zug

I. Zug

II. Zug

III. Zug

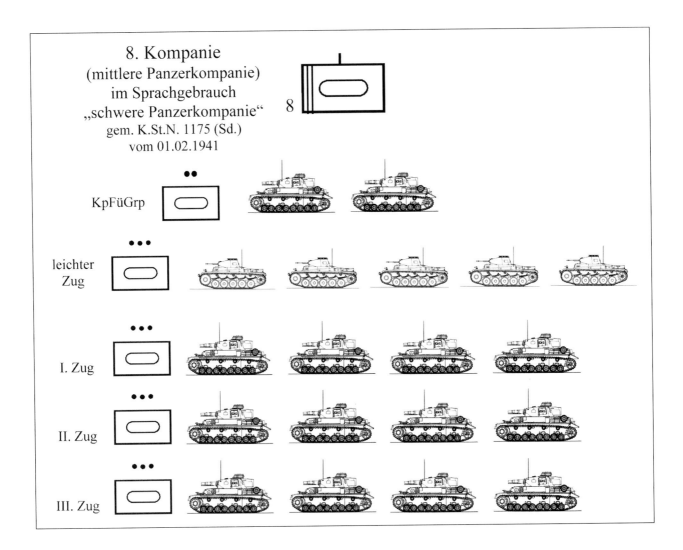

8. Kompanie
(mittlere Panzerkompanie)
im Sprachgebrauch
„schwere Panzerkompanie"
gem. K.St.N. 1175 (Sd.)
vom 01.02.1941

8

KpFüGrp

leichter
Zug

I. Zug

II. Zug

III. Zug

3. Organization and Strength of the Regiment for the Campaign in Africa

As was the case in France, the actual numbers of vehicles varied from the authorized ones. In addition, the regiment was still missing its 3rd and 7th Companies. The regiment's strength on 27 February 1941 was as follows.[6]

6. Author's Note: Jentz, 160.

Tank Type	On-hand Strength on 28 February 1941 (minus 3rd and 7th Companies)	Authorized Strength In Accordance with TO&E dated 1 February 1941 (minus the 3rd and 7th Companies)
Panzerbefehlswagen I	3	0
Panzerbefehlswagen III	4	6
Panzerkampfwagen I	25	0
Panzerkampfwagen II	45	49
Panzerkampfwagen III (L/42 5 centimeter main gun)	71	77
Panzerkampfwagen IV	20	30
Totals	168	162

In contrast to the *3. Panzer-Division*, *Panzer-Regiment 5* was the only tank formation in the *5. leichte Division.*

Panzertyp	Ist-Bestand PzRgt 5 am 28. Februar 1941 mit 1., 2., 4., 5., 6. und 8. Kompanie	Soll-Bestand für das PzRgt 5, ohne 3. und 7. Kp, gem. K.St.N. gültig ab 01.02.1941
PzBefWg I	3	0
PzBefWg III	4	6
Panzerkampfwagen I	25	0
Panzerkampfwagen II	45	49
Panzerkampfwagen III	71 (alle mit 5 cm KwK)	77
Panzerkampfwagen IV	20	30
	168	162

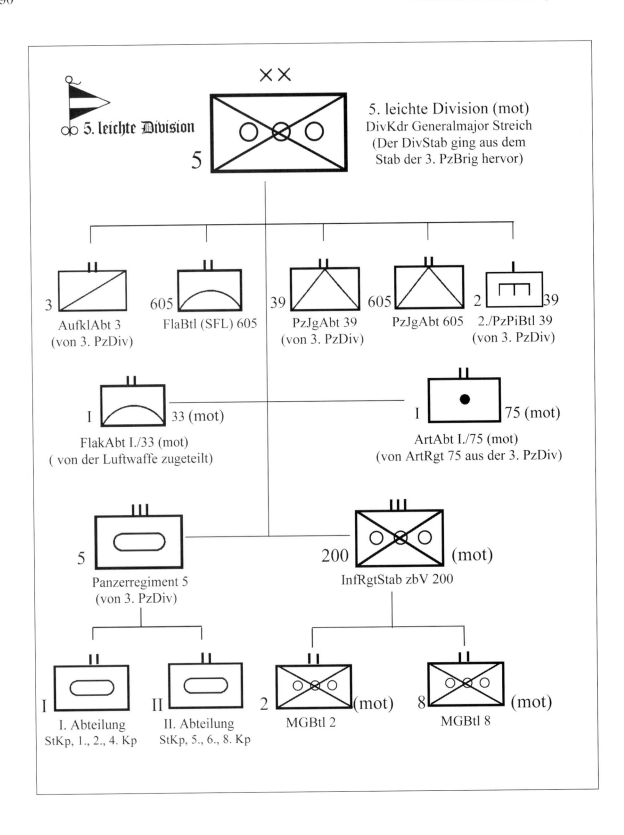

5. leichte Division

5

5. leichte Division (mot)
DivKdr Generalmajor Streich
(Der DivStab ging aus dem
Stab der 3. PzBrig hervor)

3 — AufklAbt 3
(von 3. PzDiv)

605 — FlaBtl (SFL) 605

39 — PzJgAbt 39
(von 3. PzDiv)

605 — PzJgAbt 605

2 — 39 — 2./PzPiBtl 39
(von 3. PzDiv)

I — 33 (mot) — FlakAbt I./33 (mot)
(von der Luftwaffe zugeteilt)

I — 75 (mot) — ArtAbt I./75 (mot)
(von ArtRgt 75 aus der 3. PzDiv)

5 — Panzerregiment 5
(von 3. PzDiv)

200 — (mot) — InfRgtStab zbV 200

I — I. Abteilung
StKp, 1., 2., 4. Kp

II — II. Abteilung
StKp, 5., 6., 8. Kp

2 — (mot) — MGBtl 2

8 — (mot) — MGBtl 8

4. Troop Elements of the *5. Leichte Division (mot)* on 10 February 1941 (Minus Command and Logistics Elements)

5. leichte Division

Commander: *Generalmajor* Streich

(Division headquarters and staff formed from the *3. Panzer-Brigade*)

Aufklärungs-Abteilung 3 (from the *3. Panzer-Division*)

Flak-Bataillon (Sfl) 606[7]

Panzerjäger-Abteilung 39 (from the *3. Panzer-Division*)

Panzerjäger-Abteilung 605[8]

2./Panzer-Pionier-Bataillon 39 (from the *3. Panzer-Division*)

I./Flak-Regiment 33 (mot)[9]

I./Artillerie-Regiment 75 (from the *3. Panzer-Division*)

Panzer-Regiment 5

Infanterie-Regiments-Stab zbV 200 (mot)[10]

---

7. Translator's Note: 606th Antiaircraft Battalion (Self-Propelled). The 600-level of designation indicated a general-headquarters force. It is not clear from this organization chart whether the battalion was attached to the light division or merely in direct support.

8. Translator's Note: 660th Antitank Battalion.

9. Author's Note: In direct support from the *Luftwaffe*. Translator's Note: The other antiaircraft formation was an army component.

10. Translator's Note: 200th Infantry Regiment headquarters (Special-Purpose) (Motorized). This was a separate infantry regiment headquarters command and control unit without organic forces, to which the two machine-gun battalions reported.

Maschinen-Gewehr-Bataillon 2 (mot) and *Maschinen-Gewehr-Bataillon 8 (mot)*.[11]

There has been no definitive proof of a divisional insignia for the *5. leichte Division*.[12] Some of the vehicles of the regiment, as well as the other formations that originally came from the *3. Panzer-Division*, bore the divisional insignia of their original formation, which had been changed after the campaign in the West. At the beginning of 1941, the design was as follows:[13]

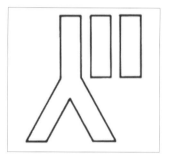

---

11. Translator's Note: 2nd and 8th Machine-Gun Battalions (Motorized).

12. Author's Note: Schmitz and Thies, *Die Truppenkennzeichen*, Vol. I, *The Army*, 663. Hereafter referred to as Schmitz.

13. Author's Note: Schmitz, 543.

A *Panzer II* of the 2nd Company on the sea journey from Naples to Tripoli in March 1941. It still has the insignia of the *3. Panzer-Division*.

Regimental pennant in black-pink-black.

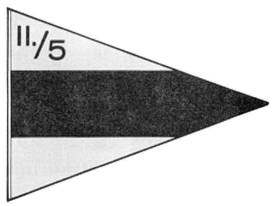

Pennant for the 2nd Battalion: Pink-black-pink. (The 1st Battalion was analogous.)

Preparing their *Panzer IV* for new operations. The crew still wears the "continental" *Panzer* uniform, soon to be replaced by items designed for wear in tropical climates.

Rail transport to Naples. The rail car of the train commander and the train guards.

The German soldiers were greeted at the railway stations by women with baskets of fruit. As a token of appreciation, other soldiers and airmen from previous transports have left souvenirs for the women.

4 March 1941: Waiting to be loaded on ships at the Naples Harbor.

The 8th Company is loaded out.

A wheeled vehicle from the regiment is loaded aboard. The *JR* stands for *Instandsetzung Regiment*, a regimental maintenance asset.

A *Panzer III* from the 5th Company is raised by the cranes. A crewmember and dock workers help steady the vehicle.

A *Panzer III* from the 6th Company onboard its tranport.

A *Panzer I* of the regimental headquarters boards the *Kybfels.*

10 March 1941: Unloading in Tripoli.

A *Panzer II* of the regimental headquarters performs guard duty during the sea transport. Since Axis control of the seas was by no means assured, the soldiers all wear life vests.

CHAPTER 6

Panzer-Regiment 5 in the Campaign in North Africa, 1941

1. 28 February to 30 March 1941: Transfer to North Africa and Defense of Tripolitania

At the beginning of February 1941, Rommel was promoted to *Generalleutnant*. He received the mission to reinforce the Italian defenses by reinforcement through German forces in the Buerat-Sirte area, around 300 kilometers southeast of Tripoli. The orders from the Army High Command read, in part:

It is imperative to bring the motorized British formations to a standstill and defeat them through offensive employment of the armored forces.[1]

Rommel is considered to be a military phenomenon in terms of bravery, audacity and dynamism. In addition, he is considered to be a master tactician.

1. Author's Note: Aberger, 24.

On 16 February 1941, *Generalleutnant* Rommel was given overall command of the German and Italian forces in the vicinity of the front.

He understood how to successfully employ armored fighting forces by exploiting their mobility and the element of surprise. He did not avoid risk, made rapid, unconventional decisions and was a master of improvisation. He led from the front and was therefore in the position to react immediately and flexibly to changes in the situation. Rommel demanded much from his men and his commanders, but he also demanded the utmost of himself. He eventually was promoted to *Generalfeldmarschall* and became one of the most famous general officers of the Second World War. His name has become symbolic of the struggle of the German soldier in Africa.

✠

By the same token, it should and must be mentioned that there were also some reservations concerning his qualities as a person and as a leader. *Oberleutnant* Harald Kuhn, a company commander in the regiment, wrote the following in his memoirs:[2]

> Undoubtedly, Rommel appeared before us as a personality.[3] Everything about him was out of the ordinary: His personal courage, his energy level, his imagination, his military good fortune but also his need to be in control, his ambition and the ruthlessness with which he brought those qualities to bear. The self-indulgence of that type of personality also brings great danger with it. If it does not succeed in establishing a basis of trust between it and its surroundings, it becomes all too easily arrogant, impatient, distrustful, unjust and—lonely. Overestimating oneself and arbitrariness seldom allow a relationship of trust develop and lead to the loss of a clear view of reality.
>
> Whenever Rommel toured the battlefield as cool as a cucumber between Tobruk and the Sollum Front in a *Fieseler-Storch*,[4] even though the airspace was swarming with English fighters, or whenever he was to be found in even the most dangerous of situations—it was said that he had five drivers shot out next to him in his vehicle—and we saw how his energy level never wore down, we admired and respected that . . .
>
> Whenever we saw and heard that Rommel preferred to be far to the front on days of combat in order to direct individual tanks and assault detachments, instead of making decisions in his headquarters, which the overall situation demanded, or when he once again demonstrated that he had completely underestimated or incorrectly estimated the enemy, then we asked ourselves whether he really was such a great military leader . . .

On the other hand, Rommel was of the opinion that a good knowledge of the terrain and the enemy's positions, as well as the better view of the battlefield, often decided a battle more than greater tactical ability.

On 11 February, the first German ground forces (logistical elements) reached the harbor at Tripoli. Rommel arrived on 12 February.

---

2. Author's Note: Harald Kuhn, *Die Ereignisse im Früh-jahr und Sommer 1941 in Libyens Wüste*, 67. Hereafter referred to as Kuhn.

3. Translator's Note: The original German is *Persönlichkeit*, which literally translates as personality, but usually implies much more, as in the sense of (he's a) character, personage, celebrity or, colloquially, "big shot."

4. Translator's Note: The *Fieseler Storch* was a light and unarmed single-engine utility aircraft that saw service throughout the entire war.

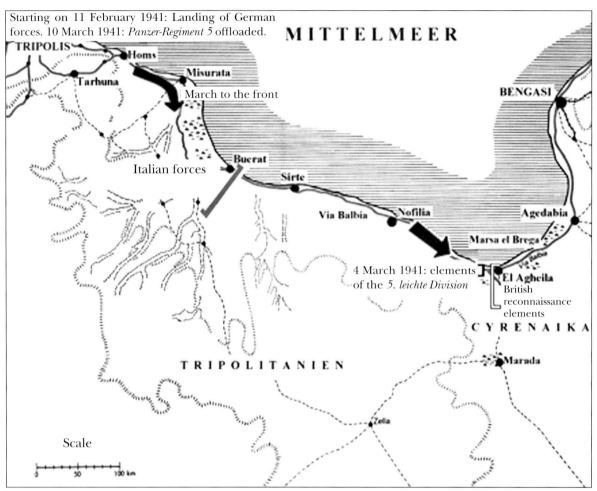

Advance of the initial elements of the *5. leichte Division* from 13 February to 4 March 1941, a distance of 600 kilometers from Tripoli to the area west of El Agheila.

On 13 February, the first combat elements of the division, *Aufklärungs-Abteilung 3 (mot)* and *Panzerjäger-Abteilung 39*, disembarked in Tripoli and were directed to the front. They reached the Buerat-Sirte area on 16 February.

Between the positions of the Axis forces in Buerat-Sirte and El Agheila was approximately 300 kilometers of no-man's-land. The English had stop their forward advance a few kilometers west of El Agheila. Rommel had a *Kampfgruppe* composed

of the reconnaissance battalion and Italian forces advance to the southeast.

On 24 February, the first enemy contact was made between reconnaissance elements on both sides in the El Agheila–Agedabia area.

The insignia of the *DAK* as applied to the right hull of the *Panzer IV* of the 2nd Platoon leader of the 8th Company.

As the result of an Armed Forces Daily Report on 26 February, the German public discovered for the first time that the German Army was conducting operations in the North African theater of war:[5]

Along the Libyan coastline southeast of Agedabia, German and English mounted patrols made contact during the morning hours of 24 February. A number of English vehicles, including a number of armored cars, were destroyed and a few prisoners taken. There were no losses on the German side . . .

By 4 March, *Panzerjäger-Abteilung 39*, reinforced by engineers, *Flak* and Italian troop elements, occupied positions 25 kilometers east of El Agheila. Without tanks and artillery, however, the prospects for continued successful operations were not realizable. For that reason, there was initially no further advance.

On 21 February, orders arrived from the Armed Forces High Command that the German forces in Africa were to be designated as the *Deutsches Afrikakorps (DAK)*. It was also announced that a complete armor division—the *15. Panzer-Division*—would also be sent to the theater in the foreseeable future to reinforce the *5. leichte Division*.[6] The insignia for the *DAK*, effective 1 April, was a stylized palm tree with a superimposed swastika.[7] It was to be added to all vehicles in addition to any formation signs.

5. Author's Note: Köhler, *Wehrmachtsberichte von den Kämpfen in Nordafrika vom 11. Januar 1941 bis 7. Februar 1942*, 5.

6. Author's Note: Aberger, 34.

7. Author's Note: Schmitz/Thies, 49.

The cuff band for members of the *DAK*, after fulfilling certain conditions (six months in theater, seriously wounded in theater, etc.) It was worn on the right sleeve, 15 centimeters above the cuff.

A few months later, the Army High Command issued a directive that the *DAK* was entitled to issue a cuff band with the lettering *Afrikakorps*. The cuff title was bordered in an olive drab with silver lettering on a dark green background.

Shown above is the Certificate of Issuance of Tropical Uniform and Equipment Articles, as issued to a soldier from the replacement detachment in Neuruppin. It is amazing how quickly the German uniform industry was able to produce large quantities of tropical clothing in such a relatively short time.

10 March 1941: The company commander's tank of the 5th Company is taken off the ship at Tripoli.

Among the items issued: 3 blankets; 2 tunics; 1 pair of boot trousers (non-mounted); 1 long pair of trousers; 1 pair of shorts (sport); 3 undershorts; 1 set of long johns; 1 overcoat; 3 olive-colored shirts; 3 undershirts; 2 night shirts; 1 scarf; 1 olive-colored tie; 1 pair of gloves; 1 olive-colored undergarment; 4 pairs of olive-colored socks; 2 pair of olive-colored calf-length socks; 1 pair of lace-up boots; 1 pair of lace-up shoes; 1 pair of suspenders; one belt; one pair of swimming trunks; 1 olive-colored pith helmet; 1 olive-colored rucksack; 1 set of load-bearing equipment; 1 mosquito mask; 1 pair of dust and sun glasses; 1 washing basin (made out of sailcloth); etc.

At the beginning of March, the regiment was transported to Africa. The sea transport across the Mediterranean proved to be difficult. After the convoy steamed out on 5 March, British naval forces were reported. The convoy docked in Palermo for 24 hours, affording the soldiers the opportunity to visit the city. On the second attempt, the convoy made it to Tripoli.

Heinz Kilanowski, a member of the 4th Company at the time and 19 years old, recalled the experience:[8]

> On 28 February 1941, *Panzer-Regiment 5* loaded out in Wünsdorf. All of the officers and enlisted personnel had been examined for tropical suitability. We crossed the Brenner Pass into Italy. In Naples, the regiment was loaded on 5 ships averaging 10,000–12,000 gross register tons. The convoy consisted of the transports *Wachtfels, Reichenfels, Acturus, Alicante* and *Leverkusen*. Italian destroyers provided escort. Between Sicily and Tripoli, we were pursued by English submarines and engaged. English submarines were waiting for us outside of Tripoli as well. The attacks were successfully turned back each time, however. On 10 March, our regiment disembarked in Tripoli.

8. Author's Note: Heinz Kilanowski in a letter to the author on 15 September 2001.

During the load-out in Naples, a fire started on the *Leverkusen*, which resulted in the loss of 10 *Panzer III's* and 3 *Panzer IV's*.[9] As a result, the following vehicles reached the port in Tripoli on 10 March: 7 *Panzerbefehlswagen*, 25 *Panzer I's*, 45 *Panzer II's*, 61 *Panzer III's* and *17 Panzer IV's*.

A parade was held in Tripoli on 12 March, followed by a road march along the coastal road—the *Via Balbia*—to the front. Over the course of 6 night marches, the regiment reached the *Arco dei Fileni*—the border marker erected by the Italians—85 kilometers southeast of Nofilia. In the area around the border marker, numerous depots for fuel, rations and ammunition were established in March with an eye towards offensive operations.

9. Author's Note: Jentz, 158.

The tanks of the 5th and 6th Companies assemble for the parade on 12 March. The crews were issued tropical clothing once they landed.

Tanks of the regiment move through the *Arco dei Fileni* on the way to the front in the second half of March.

2. 31 March to the Middle of June 1941: Recapture of Cyrenaica, Fighting for Tobruk and Operations in the Border Area between Libya and Egypt

Although the English anticipated an attack on El Agheila, they did not count on further offensive operations by the Axis powers at the time.

On 31 March, the *5. leichte Division*, initially formed into two battle groups, moved out to attack. The northern *Kampfgruppe* advanced along the coastal road through El Agheila in the direction of Marsa el Brega. The southern battle group, which included *Panzer-Regiment 5*, moved through the desert as a flank guard. The enemy was ejected from his positions and moved back in the direction of Agedabia.

During the morning of 2 April, the motorized riflemen attacked Agedabia head on, while the tanks enveloped. The envelopment took the tank regiment some 60 kilometers into the desert. Ten kilometers east of Agedabia, the regiment encountered 20 British Cruiser tanks. The regiment destroyed eight enemy tanks, losing one of its own as a complete write-off. Agedabia was taken.

The first large-scale armored engagement in Cyrenaica took place on the evening of 2 April, when 30 British tanks, including the heavily armored Mark II, the "Matilda," moved out in an immediate counterattack. After 45 minutes, the regiment was able to decide the engagement in its favor. It was shown that the German tanks had a decisive advantage as a result of their better tactics, the initiative of the individual tank commanders and their greater maneuverability. Despite that, the "Matilda" remained a feared opponent because of its heavy armor. With 8 centimeters in some locations, it was more heavily armored than any German tank of the time.

A platoon of the 8th Company during the attack on Agedabia. The desert terrain offered ideal conditions for the employment of tanks. Their maneuverability and firepower came especially to the forefront. This image demonstrates how far apart armor needed to be deployed under desert conditions.

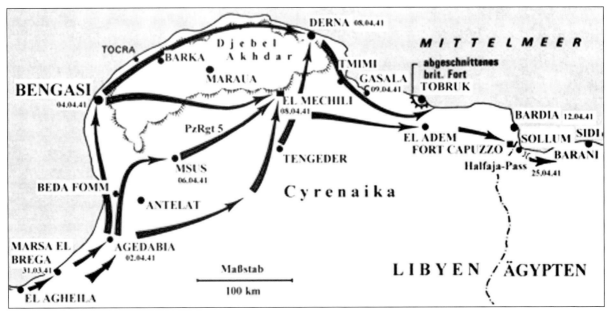

The retaking of Cyrenaica by the *5. leichte Division* and Italian forces in the spring of 1941.

On 4 April, the northern battle group occupied Bengasi, which had been evacuated by the enemy without a fight. The division then regrouped with three battle groups to continue the attack.

In the north, the reinforced *Aufklärungs-Abteilung 3 (mot)* continued along the coastal road. In the middle, the regiment, reinforced by the *I./ Artillerie-Regiment 75 (mot)* headed in the direction of Msus and, in the south, a few tanks reinforced by some motorized riflemen advanced in the direction of Tengeder. Italian forces reinforced the German formations.

On 6 April, the tank regiment took Msus and, on 8 April, El Mechili. In the taking of the desert fort, the 1st Battalion of *Major* Bolbrinker distinguished itself, with large numbers of prisoners being taken and quantities of supplies captured. Likewise, Derna fell into German hands that same day. El Mechili was the confluence of seven desert trails. From that location, the attacking forces could advance to the north in the direction of Derna, to the northeast along the coastal road in the area of Tmimi-Gazala or to the east in the direction of Tobruk-Libyan and the Egyptian frontier.

During the attack from El Agheila to El Mechili, the tank regiment suffered from a constant lack of fuel. The fuel calculated to last 500 kilometers was already used up after 170. Waiting for fuel columns, as well as breaks necessary for maintenance, slowed down the continuation of the German attack. In addition, navigation in the desert proved to be extremely difficult, since orienting features were absent and determining one's own location was only done with difficulty. Rommel, circling the advancing forces in his *Fieseler Storch*, drove his men forward and directed forces that were lagging behind. The attack was continued on a broad front between Tobruk and El Adem.

A knocked-out "Matilda." The Mark II heavy infantry tank had armor of up to 8 centimeters. It could be effectively engaged by the 8.8-centimeter *Flak* at ranges from 1,000 to 2,000 meters before it could bring its 4-centimeter main gun to bear. The 5-centimeter main gun of the *Panzer III* was only effective at ranges under 450 meters, however.

The desert fort of El Mechili was taken on 8 April.

On 9 April, Gazala was taken. The next day, Rommel's forces were at the outside defensive ring around Tobruk, where the bulk of the forces that had withdrawn from Cyrenaica had massed. The garrison of Tobruk numbered some 29,000 men in April 1941, which was numerically considerably stronger than the German forces attacking.

The attack conducted by the tank regiment through the Cyrenaican desert from 31 March to 10 April had taken a considerable toll on the operational status of the tanks, even without taking enemy action into account. An after-action report by the regiment's maintenance company from those days survived the war:[10]

> The average march distance of 700 kilometers had a very negative effect on the tanks. Up to the time when the regiment occupied its positions outside of Tobruk, the number of tanks enumerated below had to be transferred to the maintenance company on account of severe engine and/or running gear damage:
>
> 12 of 25 *Panzer I's;* 2 of 3 *kleiner Panzerbefehlswagen I's*; 19 of 45 *Panzer II's*; 44 of 65 *Panzer III's* or *Panzerbefehlswagen III's*; and 6 of 17 *Panzer IV's.*
>
> Altogether, 83 armored vehicles out of 155.
>
> The heavy damage was caused when the *Trigh el Abd*[11] was crossed at high speed, which was dictated by the tactical situation. Due to the tempo demanded, unsuitable march lengths could not be avoided. Of the 65 *panzer III's* and *Panzerbefehlswagen III's* on hand, 44 became disabled with severe engine damage during the march through the desert.
>
> The mistake was always the same. The engine lost power and the oil pressure fell to zero, whereupon the engine quit. Whenever an effort was made to continue moving after the oil had been changed, the cylinders and pistons seized. Finally, the piston rods on the third or fourth cylinder broke. The cause was the same in every case. The crankcase housing became stopped up to a paste as the result of the fine sand, whereby the transmission of the oil was interrupted. The cylinders and the pistons were worn up to 6 millimeters. Out of 83 disabled tanks, the maintenance company swapped out the engines in 58 vehicles.
>
> The available air filters are completely unsuited for the desert, since they did not restrict the fine sand. That caused the clogging of the crankcases. The use of a dry felt filter, as has been mounted on British cars, trucks and armored vehicles, is recommended.
>
> Fifty shock absorbers became unserviceable and had to be swapped out on 65 *Panzer III's* and the *Panzerbefehlswagen III's*. Twenty broken springs and 16 sets of tracks were switched on the *Panzer II's*. The problems with the springs and the shock absorbers was not only as a result of the poor route but also mines. The greasing of the auxiliary brakes as a result of the deficient brake pads was a widely encountered mistake. Sixty maintenance requests in the case of the *Panzer III's* could be traced back to bad final inspections at the factories.
>
> The ventilator shafts had to be exchanged in 40 cases, because the bearings were deficient. Problems in turret races on eight *Panzer III's* were determined to be caused by sand.
>
> Five Variorex housings had to be exchanged.

The tank regiment had only 25 operational tanks when it launched its first attack against the fortress of Tobruk from the south around 0600 hours on 11 April. More attacks would follow over the next few days.

---

10. Author's Note: Jentz, 159.

11. Translator's Note: *Trigh* is an Arabic road for path or trail.

Mine damage to a *Panzer II*.

Changing track on a *Panzer II* in Cyrenaica in April 1941.

The crew from another tank lends a hand.

Photograph from a war correspondent photographer: The first attack on Tobruk on 11 April 1941.

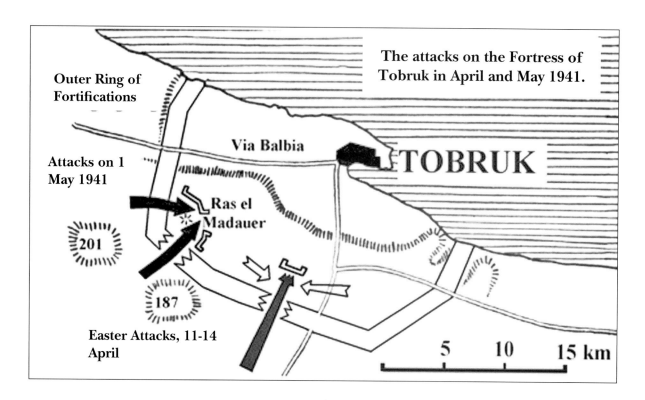

On 15 April, the operations section of the regiment compiled an after-action report on operations between 11 and 14 April:[12]

11 April 1941: At 0730 hours, the regiment received orders to attack Tobruk, enveloping from the south, advancing from 32 kilometers west of Tobruk through Acroma. The regiment moved out at 0830 hours, was received by a liaison of the *Deutsches Afrika-Korps* in Acroma, turned to the east 10 kilometers south of Acroma (based on his directives) and reached the area about 12 kilometers southwest of Tobruk around 1500 hours. The assembly area was immediately taken under artillery fire by the enemy, with the result that the element of surprise was lost.

The regimental commander was personally briefed by the commanding general. At 1600 hours, the regiment—just the headquarters and

the 2nd Battalion—moved out to attack. The regiment has been reduced to 25 vehicles. When the high ground, which could be observed by the enemy, was crossed, heavy fires commenced. The regimental attack came to an unexpected standstill as the result of an defensive ditch that could not be crossed, which went all the way around Tobruk. The regiment ordered: "Turn right and look for a passage over the ditch further east." Heavy antitank-gun fire and magnificently directed English artillery fire accompanied the regiment as it deployed and advanced 4 kilometers along the ditch. At 1715 hours, the lead elements of the regiment reached the Tobruk–El Adem road, where a thick belt of mines was identified. The regiment ordered: "Turn south; pull back from the enemy." It conducted further reconnaissance to the east by the 1st Platoon of the 2nd Battalion. In the course of the reconnaissance, which extended into the night and advanced as far as 20 kilometers southeast of Tobruk, *Oberleutnant* von Hülsen demonstrated great dexterity and

12. Author's Note: *Panzer-Regiment 5*, Operations Section, Regimental Command Post, Signed by *Oberst* Olbrich, Authenticated by *Oberleutnant* Rocholl, Regimental Adjutant.

clear thinking. The regiment returned to its lines of departure and oriented once again towards Tobruk. The enemy situation had been presented to the regiment in such a fashion that it was anticipated that he would withdraw when a German tank attack was rolling. The regiment knew nothing of either the ancient Italian tank ditch or of the large numbers of English artillery and antitank guns on hand.

12 April 1941: A engineer officer reported that there was supposedly no tank ditch 4 kilometers west of the breakthrough point identified for the regiment on 11 April. Based on that reconnaissance, the regiment was sent to that position at 1515 hours and moved out to attack with 24 vehicles. The English artillery started firing with terrific precision into the ranks of the regiment as early as its approach march halt to reorganize for the attack. At the same time, it was bombed with heavy bombs.

An engineer platoon was attached to the regiment for the attack in case there was actually a tank ditch present it could blow in the walls under the covering fires of the regiment.

As the regiment advanced, the enemy fire intensified to the extent that the engineers were unable to follow the regiment, despite their aggressive movements. At 1600 hours, the lead elements were able to positively identify the enemy field positions. At 1645 hours, the first elements of the regiment reached the tank ditch, which also proved to be non-crossable at this location as well. Artillery and antitank guns fired at the regiment over open sights, which initially remained in place, returned fire and waited for the arrival of the engineers. After they had not arrived after about 15 minutes, the regiment ordered: "Pull back from the enemy." The withdrawal took place in good form, accompanied by English artillery fire.

14 April 1941: After a fake demolition of the tank ditch by the engineers took place during the night of 12–13 April along the western portion of the English positions around Tobruk, a bridgehead was formed during the evening of 13 April by *MG-Bataillon 8* and engineers at the fork in the road 7 kilometers south of Tobruk, in which crossings over the tank ditch were created for the later crossing of the regiment. The regiment, with the attached *Panzerjäger-Abteilung 605* and the *1./Flak-Regiment 33* in direct support, was directed to close on the bridgehead by 0230 hours and move out, initially north to attack Point 99, at 0430 hours. It was anticipated for the continuation of the attack that the 1st Battalion, with the attached *Panzerjäger-Abteilung 605*, be moved forward against the withdrawing enemy as far as the *Via Balbia*, oriented to the west. The other battalion was to turn east towards Tobruk.

The enemy was already firing final protective fires as the regiment was closing, but he was unable to inflict any losses. The regiment crossed the line of departure in waves at the bridgehead 4 kilometers west of the initially designated breakthrough point at 0430 hours with 38 tanks, the 2nd Battalion in the lead, the 1st Battalion following. Three guns of *Panzerjäger-Abteilung 605* were behind the 1st Battalion. As the first wave engaged the enemy, *MG-Bataillon 8* advanced against the enemy with only 2½ platoons instead of 300 men.

The situation appeared to develop favorably; the enemy was surprised. The contact between the advancing tanks and the motorized riflemen was still intact by 0530 hours. When it started to dawn, however, antitank-gun and artillery fire descended on the regiment from all sides. The motorized riflemen bogged down. At 0600 hours, the regiment crossed Point 99, so as to advance on the *Via Balbia*. It was all on its own, 6 kilometers deep in enemy territory. The regiment received direct artillery fire from Fort Solaro, the area east of Point 99 and the area around Fort Airenti. To the right and left in the rear, the enemy moved forward with antitank guns against the point of penetration. The regiment had to defend on all sides. At the same moment, six enemy fighters came racing in on a low-level attack. Enemy bombers dropped heavy bombs. In that very uncomfortable situation, approximately 14 enemy tanks attacked from the right rear, among which were two positively identified Mark II's (heavy infantry tanks). The regiment ordered those tanks attacked, with the 1st battalion attacking head on and the 2nd Battalion enveloping to the right. During that engagement, the enemy antitank guns continued to be constantly reinforced.

The impacting shells, the burning tanks and the hissing main-gun rounds greatly hindered the regiment's visibility. When the loss of friendly vehicles had exceeded the bounds of what was acceptable by a considerable margin, the regiment decided to retreat. In good form, firing to all sides, recovering the wounded and the dead from knocked-out tanks, the regiment pulled back. When the point of penetration, which had been reoccupied by the enemy, was reached at 0800 hours, enemy antitank guns moved up again and fired, together with well-camouflaged machine guns, against the tanks moving through the bottleneck. The 200 prisoners that had been taken, who were receiving fire from their comrades, threw themselves to ground, jumped into the trenches and were lost to the regiment. Several German soldiers sitting outside the tanks were wounded or killed. The regiment used the 1st Battalion to cover the retreat through the bottleneck against the antitank guns and machine guns. The heavy, well-aimed artillery fire of the enemy followed the regiment until about 2 kilometers from the point of penetration. The regiment reassembled there, reorganized its formations and prepared to interdict a possible English pursuit, which did not take place, however. The enemy only advanced to the point of penetration with his own armored vehicles. The enemy intelligence that had been announced prior to the attack stated that the enemy was in the process of "taking down his fortifications" that his artillery was very weak and that his morale was low.

Prior to the start of the attack, the regiment knew not the slightest of the excellently constructed field fortifications, of the individual battery positions nor the unbelievably numerous antitank guns. The presence of strong enemy armor forces was also not known. The regiment moved out into the fight firmly convinced and with unshakeable will to defeat the enemy and take Tobruk. Only the vastly superior enemy, the tremendous casualties and the lack of any type of combat support caused the regiment to bend.

38 armored fighting vehicles went into the fight.

17 armored fighting vehicles were destroyed by the enemy.

2 officers are missing; 7 wounded.

21 noncommissioned officers and enlisted personnel are missing.

10 noncommissioned officers and enlisted personnel are wounded.

That comes to 50% in losses.

/signed/ Olbrich

The after-action report of the regiment above is supplemented by the firsthand account of *Oberleutnant* Harald Kuhn, who participated in the fighting as a company commander in the 2nd Battalion:[13]

Good Friday, 11 April. According to Rommel's own words, he wants to march into Cairo in a few days. We still do not know him well enough to know how good his judgment of the enemy is. And so, what does Tobruk mean to us? We will overrun it, just like we did Bengasi and Derna. There can't be much with the facilities, which are entered on the maps as a fortress, especially

---

13. Author's Note: Kuhn, 30 ff.

since they had been built by the Italians. We experienced a few weeks ago how they were unable to hold out more than a day during their flight. Based on Rommel's demand to our regiment to hurry up, there can't be too much ahead.

Without any worries, we set out during the morning with the pitiful remnants of the 2nd Battalion, so as to attack through *MG-Bataillon 8* through Acroma from the south. We were greatly surprised to start receiving raging artillery fire as we approached about 20 kilometers from the city. We were speechless when the machine-gun battalion, which was attacking ahead of us, was forced to ground, motionless, after a very short time in a murderous hail of fire.

The desert spread out in front of us, gray yellow and dead. But there were countless eyes hidden there, along with firing batteries. How was that possible? Were the fortifications going to be a difficult nut to crack after all? Rommel must have buoyed up his confidence based on something.

The grenadiers dug in, and then we advanced. One artillery shell next to the other. Dust and dirt swirled around us and made it impossible to identify neighboring vehicles. Terrific fields of vision allowed Tommy to follow every one of our movements in that hellfire.

After feeling our way forward a bit, we arrived at a broad tank ditch that was heavily wired and mined. Behind it, we could see bunkers and heavily improved field fortifications, which could barely be made out, since they barely rose above the earth. There's no getting through!

We moved along that obstacle for 3 or 4 kilometers, always pursued by artillery fire, always looking for a way to get through, before we had to turn back, our business unfinished.

The first setback. It's nothing you like to experience, especially when it comes so un-expectedly!

On Easter Saturday, a second attack in the same manner. This time, we took along engineers, who were supposed to blow a lane through the obstacle. Bombs rained down on us from the air; the same hail of shellfire. The engineers were unable to get to the obstacle and we turned back with unfinished business again.

And so that doesn't look like it'll work either. Remnants of a division, which was never an attack division with the appropriate weapons; instead, it was a blocking formation—after 1,400 kilometers of offensive operations, torn up by the pathless desert. We need more here than being cheeky and a sense of superiority. We are in need of systematic reconnaissance and well-planned employment in view of our modest means. Because the English are appearing to now start acting decisively and have effective means at their disposal.

Despite all that, Rommel has set the third attack for Easter Monday. An attack group has been formed from the 2nd Battalion of our regiment and the rest of *MG-Bataillon 8* in the first wave; behind us, the rest of the 1st Battalion, which has arrived in the meantime, the regimental headquarters, the antitank troops and the *Flak* forces.

"Don't take the tanks to the buildings of the city; leave that to the infantry!" Rommel said that to my regimental commander, who was designated to lead the attack group.

While we are getting ready, I encounter serious, taciturn faces, in which doubts on the success of the operation were mirrored. The difficult experience of the last two attacks still had us in its grip. But there was no dodging fate; we were soldiers.

We moved out at night at 0030 hours. The engineers worked their way silently forward to the obstacle. At 0100 hours, still outside of the obstacles, there was a murderous blast, and my vehicle leapt into the air, almost throwing me out of the turret. Mine! Badly knocked about, we hobbled forward with a cracked drive sprocket and ripped-off mudguards. A shock in the morning hours.

A short while later, our small group started to waver; they were looking for the prepared lane ahead. That was not so easy in the pitch-black night. Suddenly, contact was lost between the battalion commander's vehicle and the rest of the battalion. Whispered calls . . . strained listening . . . a feeling of helplessness. In the end, I was sent forward in my vehicle to reestablish contact. A comical feeling . . . playing boy scout in the dark between mines right next to the enemy!

Behind me were a few more vehicles; we thus searched in vain back and forth. The enemy heard us; his antitank guns barked. The rounds zinged past us with white tails. Occasionally, pyrotechnics arced skyward with a jagged shine. But the darkness covered us and protected us. It also did not allow us to find the breakthrough point we were seeking. It was not until it finally started to turn light in the east that I finally discovered it.

In the meantime, the forward elements were way ahead of us. The English had put their heads down and allowed themselves to be overrun.

We raced through the terrain of the fortified area, fired at on both the left and the right, so us to reestablish contact. At the same time, we took pains to follow the tracks because of the danger of mines. Pyrotechnic signals and radio calls helped give me the direction. Hits were frequently scored against the vehicle.

About half an hour went by before we finally reached the 1st Battalion; it was almost light. We needed the morning light to get oriented and fight, but the enemy was allowing us to fully deploy first.

And, unfortunately, he proved to be the stronger one. His uncounted observers directed the massed steamroller of the oppressive Tobruk artillery on us. The unarmored heavy and light

Flak had not been following us for some time—knocked out or disabled.

To the front, left and right, the resistance stiffened crazily; from behind, English tanks enveloped; the artillery fire became more and more insane; on top of everything else, the Royal Air Forces also attacked! The muzzle flashes blazed away on all sides and the hits smacked against our tanks; the mounted infantry were swept off by the row. All of us were in a trap. Haze, muck and dirt took away our visibility and, with it, fields of fire and orientation. The companies broke apart; there was no longer any deliberate attack. Everyone had his hands full, just keeping the enemy off his back.

Then—misfire in my main gun. A short while later, in the machine gun as well. All efforts to eliminate the problem proved fruitless. Condemned to defenselessness, I attempted to make sense of what was going on around me. A large portion of our vehicles were on fire; a few were still moving about and firing, on fire themselves. It was a terrible, unforgettable picture!

Could Hell be any worse? No one knew how much time had passed. Had it been hours? Minutes? We no longer had a sense for it.

It seemed to take forever until we fought our way back to the point of penetration and slowly came out of the fire beyond. Among the tanks that returned there was not a single one that did not bring considerable scars with it. Shocked, we determined how many of our comrades were missing. The casualties were horrific. A few tears left their traces in the gray, dust-encrusted faces. Was it the sadness felt for lost comrades? Was it the shock of the last few hours? Was it rage? No one said it.

Gradually, the cramped feeling loosened up and we turned to thoughts of what was immediately important. The old vets from the First War claimed they had never experienced a blacker day. The younger ones believed them.

So . . . after we learned to appreciate the strength of the fortress after the first two attacks, we hoped that Rommel had learned as well. Maps were finally printed and distributed in the division, where the defensive positions were marked. Finally, after we had had to pay for the lesson in looking at them with much treasure. Finally, even though our allies had constructed the fortifications, we had to capture an Italian map from the English to have it reproduced! Tobruk was surrounded by three heavily improved belts of fortifications: Concrete bunkers and trenches, wire obstacles, mines, minefields, heavily fortified field positions, numerous strong forts. The fortification belts extended with radii of about 16, 10 and 5 kilometers around the city and harbor. To the untrained eye, nothing stood out. All of the facilities were in the earth and cleverly adopted and camouflaged to the terrain. Even from the air, very little could be made out. Later on, it was said that Tobruk was the most

modern system of fortifications in the world. At the very least, it had made us all very thoughtful individuals!

Whenever we considered that the possession of the harbor meant everything to the British for their supplies and that, in addition, Tobruk was the last bulwark before the frontier with Egypt, then we understood why it was defended with any and all means and with extreme stubbornness. If they did not fix us there, then there was no longer any opportunity to do so before Egypt.

All of the remaining forces were brought forward, including the Italians, so as to place a siege ring around the city. At the very least, all land communications were intended to be disrupted. Our air force was to monitor the harbor and make it impossible to use.

My regiment was given an area to the south of the city, to which the immobilized vehicles also had to be towed to be placed into position. No main gun, no machine gun could be left behind.

A knocked-out *Panzer III* burns out.

The few operational tanks were consolidated into "hunting parties" so as to interdict any breakout attempts on the part of the Tommies and overwatch a 17-kilometer gap in the front to the right of our sector, which could not be occupied due to a lack of forces.

There was a transition to the defense all along the line.

While the division attacked Tobruk, its reconnaissance battalion, *Aufklärungs-Abteilung 3 (mot)*, continued advancing east. On 12 April, Bardia was taken. After turning back a British counterattack on 22 April at Capuzzo, the battalion continued east to the border of Libya and Egypt and advancing to the Halfaya Pass area by 25 April. For Rommel, Tobruk was a thorn in his side. The enemy fortress interrupted the important coastal road for the resupply of the Axis forces, which were brought forward some 1,400 kilometers from Tripoli. The bypass around Tobruk lengthened the journey by another 75 kilometers of tiresome desert marching, which not only led to a loss of time but also additional wear and tear on vehicles before the logistics could reach the forces positioned along the border.

As a result, Rommel attempted to take Tobruk again in May. During April, elements of the *15. Panzer-Division* had arrived in Africa: *Panzerjäger-Abteilung 33*, *Kradschützen-Bataillon 15*, elements of *Schützen-Regiment 104* and *Schützen-Regiment 115*, *Pionier-Bataillon 33* and the *I./Flak-Regiment 18*. Those formations were committed to the fighting at Tobruk. Elements of four divisions—the *5. leichte Division*, the *15. Panzer-Division*, the Italian *Ariete* Armor Division and the Italian *Brescia* Infantry Division—attacked Tobruk from the southwest on the morning of 1 May. The main effort of the attack focused in the *Ras el Madauer* hill mass.

Once again the outer defensive ring was penetrated, a number of concrete positions taken and the high ground captured, but the attacking force then reached its culminating point. Rommel ordered the attack called off.

Leutnant Schorm of the 6th Company of the regiment recounted his experiences surrounding the attack on 1 May in his diary:[14]

We planned on taking Tobruk. My 4th attack on the city. First call at 0330 hours. Departure at 0430 hours. We lost contact in the darkness and the dust, but then we were able to reestablish contact. We moved through the bottleneck in which so many of our comrades had already fallen. Then we deployed—the 6th Company on the left, the 5th Company on the right, the headquarters behind it, 8th and 7th Companies. The regiment is now being led by Hohmann and consisted of the 5th Company (formerly the 1st and 2nd Companies), the 6th Company (5th and 6th Companies), the 7th Company (those that remain) and the 8th Company (4th and 8th Companies)—in all, 80 tanks.

The British artillery started firing on us all of a sudden. We attacked. No German patrols had been sent out ahead of us. One row of cannon after the other appeared in front of us in the triangular field fortifications. The two light platoons of the company and my section were directed to attack from the flank. I attacked. A radio message stated that the company commander of the 6th Company had been hit in the tracks. Then everything happened very quickly. A terrible crash from the right. Artillery? No. It must have been a mine. A rapidly dispatched radio message: "Schorm ran over a mine; attempting to move back in own tracks." Five meters to the rear, then a new explosion—this time, to the left. It was all

---

14. Author's Note: Jentz, 163.

over with attempting to move. Another radio message: "Ran over another mine when pulling back. Moving to Tank 623." 100 meters back through artillery fire—made it.

Radio orders: "Tanks pull back behind the ridgeline." Considering the circumstances, things went well for the men in the "mine tank." The enemy attacked with tanks but was defeated in the engagement.

Moved back carefully. I then screened north along with the last tank of the company and *Leutnant* Rocholl. 9 *Panzer III's* and 3 *Panzer II's* of the 6th Company had to be abandoned due to mine damage. In my platoon: The platoon leader's tank and the two tanks of the section leader. It goes without saying that the enemy continued to fire on us for some time.

A slight change in position: forwards and to the right—to the rear and left! When the company commander arrived, I was directed forward along with *Leutnant* Dim to recover tanks. While we

Hauptfeldwebel Wilhelm Wendt, the First Sergeant of the 5th Company of the regiment, was simultaneously employed as the platoon leader of the 1st Platoon when the designated platoon leader was no longer available. He later received the Knight's Cross to the Iron Cross on 30 June 1941.

were moving, we received fire from a distance of 550 meters from machine guns and antitank guns. I silenced them with high-explosive rounds and moved backwards in the tracks of Tank 624. Then the tiresome recovery work started. The antitank-gun fire started up again and had to be contained by continuous machine-gun fire from *Leutnant* Dim. In the process, *Leutnant* Dim also rolled over a mine and sustained track damage. Finally, I started moving away from there with 624 in tow. Through a gap and then another 800 meters.

250,000 *Mark* were saved. The crew was really relieved to have its tank back again. Further back to the battalion. It was late in the afternoon by then.

Dive bombers and two-engined bombers attacked the enemy continuously. Despite that, the Britons conducted repeated immediate counterattacks with tanks. As soon as the aircraft disappeared, the artillery commenced with savage fire.

It started to turn dark. Who was enemy and who was friends? Rounds were fired all over the place, frequently against friendly forces and on tanks employed up front that were on their way back.

Suddenly, radio traffic! The Britons were attacking the gap with infantry. It was true. 2 companies dismounted from their vehicles. All sorts of pyrotechnics climbed into the skies— green, red, white. Flares hissed down in the vicinity of our machine guns. It was already too dark to aim. The attack of the enemy had to have been a mistake.

The small Fiat-Ansaldo tanks with the flame-throwers moved forward to clear the triangle. Long streams of flame consisting of fuel oil, thick smoke and a terrible stink! We screened until 2345 hours and then pulled back through the bottleneck. It was a crazy movement through the dirt clouds. At 0300 hours, I had a quick bite to eat next to the tank. Locked up inside the tank for 24 hours—with terrible pain in my limbs and muscle cramps as a consequence, not to mention an unbelievable thirst!

Hauptfeldwebel Wilhelm Wendt wrote about his experiences during the fighting on 1 May:

> During the early-morning hours of 1 May, I was attached to the 2nd Company with my platoon. We attacked without delay in the direction of Tobruk, through a gap created by the engineers. After about 3 kilometers, I ran over two mines, one after the other. I then understood what the small piles of rocks that were painted white on the enemy side meant: Careful! Minefield! My driver reported to me that the tank would no longer move forward. I jumped out of my tank to see what kind of track damage had been sustained. I attempted to warn the entire company by radio so it would avoid the same fate, but it was too late. Of the 22 tanks of the company, only 2 made it through the minefield unscathed. Under heavy artillery fire, I ran back to warn the other elements of the company of the minefield so that no further unnecessary losses took place.
>
> I received the mission from the company commander, *Oberleutnant* Grün, to get all of the tanks that were immobilized in the minefield moving again as much as possible. Under heavy antitank-gun and artillery fire, one tank after the other in the minefield was made mobile enough again that it could roll back to the rearward maintenance services. In the process, I always had two tank crews provide alternating covering fire during the recovery in order to hold down a field position in front of us through their fires.
>
> In the course of the mission, which was conducted under the baking summer heat, my comrades came to me and stated they were no longer in a position to continue working because of their thirst. I decided to have radiator water drained so as to still the thirst. You really had to have drunk one of those "radiator water cocktails" at some point in time to know what miserable swill that radiator broth was. In any event, their thirst was gone, although a portion had a strange rumbling in their stomachs and others had to take a trip with a spade more often than was their norm! Towards 1600 hours, I had accomplished my mission to the extent that all but a few tanks were able to roll back at a snail's pace to the maintenance services.
>
> The entire attack failed after several days, with the result that the troop elements were directed back to their sectors around the ring encircling Tobruk.

In the days that followed, the German forces in the bridgehead around the *Ras el Madauer*—7 kilometers wide by 3 kilometers deep—had to turn back numerous British counterattacks. That was followed by positional warfare for the next few months, with its corresponding attrition and casualties. The prerequisite for maintaining a siege of Tobruk was holding the positions in the area of the Libyan-Egyptian border and the Halfaya Pass. The Halfaya Pass was of additional importance for the British because it allowed movements in the direction of Capuzzo from the coastal plain across the mountains to the desert area, thus eliminating time-robbing movements through the desert.

As a result, the main effort of the fighting shifted to the Libyan-Egyptian border in the area of Sollum and the Halfaya Pass. In order to reinforce the German forces employed there, elements of the *15. Panzer-Division* were dispatched, as well as the 2nd Battalion of the regiment under *Major* Hohmann.

The English had the intention of delivering a short, sharp blow to the *DAK* that same May, before all of the *15. Panzer-Division* had arrived at the front. The Commander-in-Chief of the British forces, General Wavell, ordered an attack on the Halfaya Pass, Sollum and Capuzzo.

On 15 May, Operation "Brevity" started, employing approximately 100 newly arrived British tanks. It took Halfaya Pass and Capuzzo. The next day, Capuzzo was lost again, when formations of the *15. Panzer-Division*, including the recently introduced *Panzer-Regiment 8*, counterattacked. On 20 May, *Generalmajor* von Ravenstein was designated as the new commander of the *5. leichte Division.*

The *DAK* ordered *Operation "Skorpion"* to retake the Halfaya Pass. On the morning of 27 May, an attack was launched by both *Panzer-Regiment 5* and *Panzer-Regiment 8*, which was successful. *Hauptfeldwebel* Wendt, still employed as both a platoon leader and the First Sergeant of the 5th Company, experienced the attack as follows:

> The 5th Company of *Panzer-Regiment 5* was employed as the lead company of the 2nd Battalion. I led the 1st Platoon; the two other platoons were deployed to the right and left of the 1st Platoon on a broad front. My company commander, *Oberleutnant* Gierga, had already asked the battalion several times whether an attack was finally going to take place. The request was always turned down . . . finally, the company commander acted on his own. His order to the company went something like this: "Wendt, attack head on with your platoon; the two other platoons envelop to the right and left!"
>
> At about 2,000 meters there was an English *Ratsch-Bum*[15] battalion with 16 guns in position,

which were constantly taking us under fire. For me, there was only one option. It was to advance on the enemy—more properly, into the enemy—as fast as possible. I kicked my driver, *Unteroffizier* Raadts, in the back and ordered him to move even faster. He shot back: "I'm already doing 43 . . . there's no going any faster!"

At 800 meters, I took another firing halt to hold down the enemy. Racing ahead, we entered the enemy artillery position to overrun it. I was moving about 300 meters ahead of my platoon and saw a loader on the English guns carry a shell to the piece when I was about 100 meters away. I thought to myself: Get ready, you're about to make your maker! My crew probably thought the same thing. Having approached to within 30 meters of the first gun, I saw the muzzle flash and immediately felt a hard blow against the armor. For a few seconds, I was mentally dead. The tank continued to roll, however, into the enemy position, even though the driver was no longer thinking about giving it gas. I overcame the shock immediately and asked to anyone listening: "What happened?" No one answered, however.

I then addressed each of my comrades in turn and each confirmed that nothing had happened. I looked out of the turret to get a take on the situation and immediately came to the decision to jump down from the tank to wave over the confused English soldiers to my tank as prisoners. After all, the crews on the English guns must have also been just as perplexed and looked at my actions as the charge of the devil, since they were no longer capable of taking any action.

A gun somewhat off to the side attempted to take flight by moving out quickly, but my wonderful gunner, *Unteroffizier* Thomm ("Tommi") fired it up immediately with a round that hit. The crews only came hesitantly to my tank. I grabbed

---

15. Translator's Note: The soldier jargon of *Ratsch-Bum* was usually applied to the Soviet 7.62-centimeter antitank gun, so named because the sound of its report and its impact were nearly simultaneous.

one of the Englishmen, who attempted to hide beneath the limber of his gun, by the seat of his pants and attempted to pull him up. He then knew what was what and immediately made some gestures that he really had to have something to drink first. I directed him to my tank, where he immediately had some peppermint tea that had been boiled out of salt water. To this day, I still do not like peppermint tea, since that slippery taste is still in my mouth.

Everything then transpired in a manner that was neither obvious nor fast. The engineer platoon took the prisoners and the spoils-of-war. The hit, that I had received, was, fortunately, on a spare roadwheel that we always had on the front slope of the tank behind the spare track. As a result, the shell had lost most of its effectiveness. Only the headlights on the outside were shattered. On the inside, the radio equipment was no longer completely intact. In the meantime, my company commander, *Oberleutnant* Gierga, had arrived. I orally reported the completion of my mission. He just said: "Top, I already saw you in heaven!" My answer: "I was mentally already with St. Peter, but I'm still here." Later on, I was awarded the Iron Cross, First Class, for my actions.

Following those attacks, a strongpoint defense was established by the *15. Panzer-Division*. The forces of the *5. leichte Division*, which had been employed in the siege ring were relieved by Italian formations. The division became the corps reserve and occupied an assembly area northwest of El Adem. The tank regiment remained with the division. The Italians constructed a 75-kilometer-long bypass route, the "Axis Road," which allowed logistics to flow to the Sollum Front around the beleaguered Tobruk.

3. 15–17 June 1941: The Battle of Sollum (Operation "Battleaxe")

The failure of Operation "Brevity" in May did not keep the English from planning to attack the Axis forces again in June. To that end, the English assembled 300 Mark II's and Mark IV's of the 7th Armoured Division and 25,000 men of the Indian 4th Infantry Division. Operation "Battleaxe" started on 15 June with attacks on Halfaya Pass, the Capuzzo area and Sollum.

The first attacks on Capuzzo were turned back by 8.8-centimeter *Flak* and elements of *Panzer-Regiment 8*, under the command of *Hauptmann* Johannes Kümmel, thereafter called the "Lion of Capuzzo." The continued British attacks led to the capture of the town, however, as well as Musaid and Strongpoint 206. The key terrain of Strongpoint 208 and, above all, Halfaya Pass—defended by the *I./Schützen-Regiment 104* under *Hauptmann* Bach—withstood all attacks. The English took heavy losses in tanks, which depreciated their over-all offensive combat power decisively.

The division, which had been the corps reserve up to that point and held in the area around Tobruk, was moved to the Sidi Azeiz area the evening of 15 June. Rommel ordered an attack on 16 June from Sidi Azeiz, swinging out through Sidi Omar and landing in the rear of the enemy at Sidi Suleiman.

Once again, *Hauptfeldwebel* Wendt was there:

During the early-morning hours of 16 June, *Panzer-Regiment 5* was employed for the first time against the English positions in the direction of Sidi Omar. After short enemy contact, orders were received to pull back. I had to relinquish leadership of the 1st Platoon to *Leutnant* Kästner, who had recovered from his wounds and returned, and served as a section leader in the platoon. It must have been around 1100 hours, when another attack was ordered. But that one was also called off after short enemy contact. We disengaged from the enemy again to occupy ambush positions in the blazing heat. No tree, no bush . . . but sun, plenty of sun!

The contours of the enemy vehicles were obscured to such an extent by the flickering heat that you could no longer tell what type of vehicle you had in front of you. During the afternoon hours—it must have been around 1600 hours— the regiment was ordered to attack again. Our 5th Company attacked in the middle of an inverted wedge, with the 1st Platoon in the middle of the company. My platoon leader, *Leutnant* Kästner, had to go to the rear, since his tank was no longer operational. The company commander transferred leadership of the platoon to me again and cursed like I had never heard him before about the somewhat hesitant attack of his company. I then attacked expeditiously with my platoon and was able to knock out several enemy tanks during a firing halt. I advanced rapidly head-on against the enemy, capitalizing on the *élan* of my cohesive crew. The English, like a swimming formation, were employed practically across our path. I stopped again and again for short firing halts, during which my gunner, "Tommi," knocked out several tanks each time to help fend off the enemy attack. We took the last firing halt about 400 meters from the enemy. I was able to observe how the enemy started to flee all of a sudden to the rear. I immediately pursued in my tank to keep on his heels. The enemy's defensive fires concentrated on my tank.

I had just given the gunner orders to continue firing while on the move, when I saw that the barrel of the main gun (5-centimeter) had a considerable kink in the middle. I then shook my gunner, grabbing him on the collar, not to fire to avoid a burst barrel. Despite that, we continued to move. We were then hit by an English antitank gun, a direct hit that penetrated. In all the excitement, I did not realize there were wounded in the tank. It was not until the tank slowed down and then came to a stop that I realized that something had to have happened. I immediately addressed my crew in general: "Did something happen?" Since I received no answer, I addressed them individually: "Tommi, did something happen?" He complained: "Ow . . . my legs, my hands hurt so much." Nothing had happened to our radio operator and loader, but our terrific driver, Opi, said nothing. I immediately jumped out of the commander's hatch so as to evacuate our gunner, *Unteroffizier* Thomm, from the tank and dress his wounds. The radio operator and loader helped me in the process. While we were applying dressings, I asked the radio operator, Hagedorn: "What's going on with Opi?" He looked and reported: "Opi won't be saying another word . . . he's dead." I was enraged and answered: "Nonsense, Opi can't be dead. Did you feel his pulse?" "No, I'll take another look." It was determined that he wasn't dead.

I ordered him to get his belt ready so we could evacuate Opi. After that had happened, my commander, *Major* Köhn, appeared and asked: "Man, Wendt, what's going on?" I cursed and told the commander: "I have two wounded in the vehicle." "Yes, but you also did it. We got through! I'll call the doc on the radio right away."

The battalion physician was at our location in short order and assumed responsibility for caring for the badly wounded. He had to remove the dressing I had put on, because I had used the most primitive of means (a chair leg). While attending to *Unteroffizier* Thomm he casually stated: "Straighten out his leg good so I can put on the splint properly. That won't hurt, after all!" At that point, *Unteroffizier* Thomm responded: "Yes, *Herr Oberarzt,* if I were Winnetou, I wouldn't be feeling any pain. But I'm not Winnetou."[16] At the same time, he saw his brother-in-arms on the stretcher and asked the physician: "Take care of our Opi first . . . he is a lot worse off than I am." That gesture was such a demonstration of comradeship that will always remain etched in my memory. I had to turn away, since that episode had stirred me so much that I could not help but cry. After being treated, both of the men were transported to the field hospital. Both healed completely.

Our successes were only possible with a crew that worked extremely well together, that trusted one another with the knowledge that only a cohesive brotherhood brings about success. After the Battle of Sollum was decided, I was asked whether I had heard the radio order to pull back from the enemy. I had to answer the question with no. My radio operator, Hagedorn, had not heard the message either. That is also the explanation for the fact that I was so far ahead of the company with my tank when I advanced by myself into the enemy . . .

16. Translator's Note: Winnetou was the fictional Indian hero of a series of western novels written by German writer Karl May, who was extremely popular in Germany.

I think about what my gunner, *Unteroffizier* Thomm, said to me once in the tank as he looked up at me: "*Herr Hauptfeldwebel*, I am really afraid. But when I see you, I no longer have any fear." But my thoughts were different: "Dear Tommi, if you only knew how fearful I am and how often, then you'd certainly lose your trust in me." But that's the way it was. You have to keep yourself in check and self-disciplined when it's a matter of life or death, so much so that it sometimes seemed that your nerves would tear you apart.

Around 0600 hours on 17 June, Sidi Suleiman was taken by the regiment, followed by *MG-Bataillon 2*, however, the machine-gun battalion was later pushed back to Sidi Omar. The German attack to the enemy's flanks and rear forced the English to pull back to the south to avoid being encircled.

Leutnant Frede, also in the 5th Company of the regiment, recalled his participation in the fighting as follows:[17]

That evening, our badly plucked *II./Panzer-Regiment 5* assembled somewhere close to the wire fence.[18] I was functioning as the signals officer in

17. Author's Note: Aberger, 70.
18. Author's Note: The Libyan-Egyptian frontier.

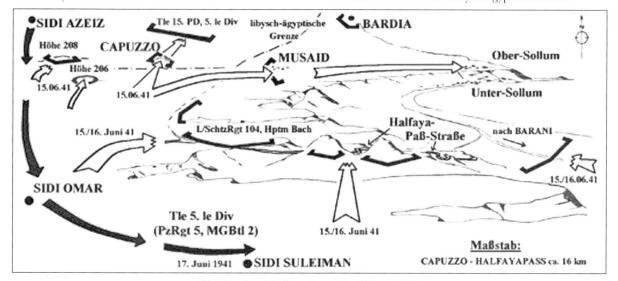

The Battle of Sollum from 15–17 June 1941

the battalion commander's tank, receiving radio traffic, which was supposed to direct the logistics units to us. The battalion commander had gone to a conference at the regiment. Suddenly, an alert: "9 Mark II's at the border fence." Apparently, they wanted to "go home."

Oberleutnant Gierga, the company commander of the 5th, issued orders: "Everyone who still has fuel and ammunition, follow me!" Nine tanks were ready to go; that meant a force ratio of 1:1. That isn't exactly true, since the command tank only had a dummy main gun made out of wood. We moved out on a board front and soon reached the enemy. The Mark II's had a top speed of only 25 kilometers an hour. Gierga had soon reached the lead elements with three tanks and found a good firing position. I headed towards the right flank. Suddenly, a black column of smoke came out of the Mark II in front of me. Apparently,

the left-hand engine had quit. The tank crew dismounted and was picked up by another tank.

The driver observed: "There're eight men in the turret, sitting there like sardines in a can. They're probably not going to fire. Perhaps we could ram their crate?" It was a tempting thought, taking a Mark II with a wooden main gun. We pressed towards the Mark II in the flank; there was a hard crash, then the tank came to a standstill. The English climbed out of the turret, somewhat battered. A senior sergeant from London saluted and said that he though it was fair that we had not engaged his overloaded tank with our main gun. We were a bit ashamed of that praise, and no one had worked up the gumption to tell him the truth.

The weak ring encircling around Sidi Omar–Sidi Suleiman was unable to prevent most of the British

Fort Capuzzo, bitterly contested in the Battle of Sollum.

forces from pulling back to Sidi Barani. It should be mentioned, however, that the 7th Armoured Division had lost more than 150 tanks, compared to a total loss of 25 tanks for the *DAK*. The Axis forces were unable to pursue, however, due to logistical issues.

"Battleaxe" had failed. The largest tank engagement in the desert up to that point had been settled in favor of the Axis, because the Germans had demonstrated superiority in the leadership of large armored formations. General Wavell had initiated the battle on Churchill's directive. He thought that with his numerically superior forces, he could destroy the *5. leichte Division* and the *15. Panzer-Division*, which had not yet completely arrived. But in the end, he lost the battle. General Auchinleck was designated as the new Commander-in-Chief for the Commonwealth forces in the Near East.

It took months before the English could replace their losses. The German defensive victory ensured that the siege of Tobruk could continue and that the front around Sollum could be stabilized.

4. Knight's Cross Recipients of *Panzer-Regiment 5* in May and June 1941

After the conclusion of the fighting, the Armed Forces Daily report announced the following on 20 June (extract):[19]

> In the fighting along the Sollum Front, the acting commander of a tank regiment, *Major* Bolbrinker . . . the company commander, *Oberleutnant* Gierga . . . distinguished themselves through their extraordinary bravery.

Major Bolbrinker, *Oberleutnant* von Senfft zu Pilsach, *Oberleutnant* Gierga and *Hauptfeldwebel* Wendt were the first four Knight's Cross recipients of the regiment, recognized for their actions in the fighting in the desert up to June 1941.

19. Author's Note: Köhler, 33.

The Knight's Cross of the Iron Cross.

The Knight's Cross of the Iron Cross was a neck order and the highest level of the Iron Cross that was reintroduced in 1939 (following the Iron Cross, Second Class, and the Iron Cross, First Class). Prerequisites for the award were:

- Exceptional personal bravery or successful combat leadership,
- A decision made on one's own initiative and
- A decisive success for the conduct of operations in general.

Of the approximately 18 million men who served in the German Armed Forces during the war, only 7,318 received the Knight's Cross.

Ernst Bolbrinker: born 1898; died 2 July 1982; submitted for the Knight's Cross on 8 May 1941; awarded the Knight's Cross on 15 May 1941 while serving as a *Major* and the commander of the 1st Battalion of *Panzer-Regiment 5*.

Ott-Friedrich von Senfft zu Pilsach: born 1913; died 1 May 1979; submitted for the Knight's Cross on 18 June 1941; awarded the Knight's Cross on 27 June 1941 while serving as an *Oberleutnant* and the commander of the 4th Company of *Panzer-Regiment 5*.

Kurt Gierga: born 1909; died 25 June 1961; submitted for the Knight's Cross on 18 June 1941; awarded the Knight's Cross on 30 June 1941 while serving as a *Hauptmann* and the commander of the 5th Company of *Panzer-Regiment 5*.

Wilhelm Wendt: born 1911; died 19 February 1984; submitted for the Knight's Cross on 18 June 1941; awarded the Knight's Cross on 30 June 1941 while serving as a *Hauptfeldwebel* and a platoon leader and first sergeant in the 5th Company of *Panzer-Regiment 5*.

5.1 September to the Middle of November 1941: Reorganization and Redesignation of the *5. leichte Division* into the *21. Panzer-Division*; the Advance South (Operation *"Sommernachtstraum"*); and a Period of Relative Rest

By the end of June 1941, the formations of the *DAK* were relieved in place in the area around Sollum by Italian forces. The German forces in the field needed a battlefield reconstitution after months of operations. The period offered a good opportunity for changes in command. As a result, the regiment received *Oberstleutnant* Stephan as its new commander at the beginning of July 1941.[20] Maintenance and servicing of the vehicles and equipment were urgently needed. Replacements that had arrived from Germany could be trained in relative quiet and incorporated into the ranks. Good news for the German forces was the large amount of spoils-of-war. English uniform items found their way into the German ranks and English vehicles supplemented the German inventory.

20. Author's Note: Kuhn, 65.

Maintenance is performed on a *Panzer III* in an assembly area. Note the supplemental track and roadwheels on the front slope. They not only provided battlefield-ready replacements, but they also afforded some additional protection for the crew.

For a while, the troops were also able to enjoy the large amount of British rations that had been captured. Once that was exhausted, it was back to the monotonous Axis fare: hard bread, cheese in tubes, canned sardines and Italian canned meat. Back then, canned sardines were something of a delicacy in Europe. In the desert, however, the warmed-up fish tasted terrible and the smell caused queasy stomachs.

The Italian canned meat was of poor quality, half of it consisting of tendons and gristle. The designation on the cans—*AM* or *administratione militare*—gave rise to a number of created substitutions for the abbreviation: *asinus Mussolini, alter Mann* ("old man"), *armer Mussolini* ("poor Mussolini), *Achsenmist* ("Axis manure") and so on.

Oberleutnant Kuhn wrote about life in the desert in his memoirs:[21]

Dear ones back home!

What kind of ideas do you entertain concerning life and activities of your men in Libya? At the beginning, I portrayed the illusions with which we headed south and how they were literally blown away. Only a few of you will be able to form an opinion from the tinted reports of the war correspondents and the descriptions given by comrades in letters that even remotely approaches the truth. Ask a member of the Africa Corps after a few years what memories have remained most alive for him: Despite the happy

21. Author's Note: Kuhn, 54.

tendency of people to quickly purge unpleasant things out of their memories, he would answer: Sandstorms, torturous swarms of flies and bleak monotony.

All of that truly not a suitable subject for a war photographer!

So that means you get pictures of palm groves, oases, camels, donkeys, Arabs or pictures of Tripoli, Bengasi or Derna that are meant to say that's our world. Not by a wide margin! The fighting soldier sees none of that or only after months, if a good or bad circumstance takes him to the rear area. For him, every day means a struggle against the adversity of this country and continuously demands anew a large measure of willpower.

When I went to our battalion physician in Derna after getting a sprained ankle after our nighttime operation on 15 May and saw the green bushes and trees and the blue sea after weeks of sand, he said to me: "You're making eyes like a young boy seeing a lit-up Christmas tree for the first time!"

Only the evening bring us some relief, when the storm settles, the flies settle down, the temperature becomes bearable and the clear sky arches above us with uncountable stars. Our eyes then search out the "Seven Sisters" that connect us with you over thousands of kilometers, and quiet, peaceful, longing thoughts grow in the immeasurable silence around us. It should be mentioned that we want those evenings to remain as unforgettable to us as the bad images of the day.

I have already described our bitterest enemy in nature, the sandstorm. A proper *ghibli* is relatively rare compared to a normal sandstorm. It can be differentiated by its direction. It comes from the south, reaches temperatures of up to 60 degrees [140 degrees Fahrenheit] and is considerably higher. If the *ghibli* blows the entire day, it is possible that it suddenly changes direction towards evening and, in the process, the temperature

changes a few degrees within a matter of minutes. Sandstorms often make visibility of more than 2 or 3 meters impossible, even in the middle of the day. As a result, combat operations are completely dependant upon them. There is no protection against the sand, even in our tents, something that can be read in the homeland newspapers.

And if no sandstorm is blowing—the worst storms end in May—then the heat plagues us. All activity ceases towards noon. Even on days of fighting, it becomes quieter around noon. Our weathermen have recorded temperatures of up to 75 degrees [167 degrees Fahrenheit]. Pieces of metal become so hot they cannot be touched and even our tireless maintenance personnel have to rest. Yes, it has even happened that uniform items left to dry on the tanks have burned up. Later on, in a newsreel back home, I saw how soldiers fried eggs over-easy on a tank that had been superheated by the sun. Those watching were happy to see how good those "down below" had it. I could have yelled in anger! Even if that event were possible, where were we supposed to get the eggs and, moreover, the grease?

Our nourishment was one of the saddest episodes of those months: Bread, leathery meat in cans—characterized accurately by our soldiers as the "old man"—or canned sardines and dried vegetables; infrequently, a lemon for fresh vitamins. Day-by-day, week-by-week, month-by-month—always the same. What we wouldn't give to have some fresh meat, vegetables or fruit, not to mention eggs! At the most, you can talk an Arab out of a couple of onions or a melon for gouge prices. In the supply depots in Bengasi and Tripoli there were better things on hand, donations form the homeland in the form of canned fruit, canned ham and other unknown pleasures—even, sparkling wine. That was being put up for better times, however, that is—the advance of the English. Then all of those phantasmagoric items were blown sky high!

In contrast, "issue" rations were transported, that is, the "old man," the canned sardines and the dried vegetables. Headline: The Management!

As part of the program of musical requests on the German Radio Network, a soldier in Africa wanted to hear a woman splashing water in a bathtub. You're laughing? The request was filled. For us, the issue of water was one of the more serious ones, not to mention that of women. For you, a toilet is a daily necessity and something you don't think about. For us here, it is a mirage. We take a shovel over our shoulders out into the desert.

But I also want to talk about potable water here. The water from Derna is famous. But it never reaches us. We scoop out of small wells that were bored with great effort that are located hours apart from one another and only provide brackish water. They are filled in large containers that have been eaten away inside with a protective coating of rust. That which we can drink after it has been boiled is a red-brown, salty, warm broth. You don't develop a thirst for it; that's the only good thing about it.

Finally, these rapes of our organisms are the cause of the occasional catastrophic status of our health. Sometimes, as many as 60% of us suffer from dysentery-like diarrhea at the same time. No one is spared. When you have it, you don't know whether you want to live or die. When you have to go down to your knees more than 70 times in a day, then to know what hit you. Colds may also be the cause of all those causes of diarrhea, since all of the colds here hit the kidneys and stomach. The daily departures for the medics often put company commanders in a tight spot when it comes to operational readiness.

In the mental picture you have formed, the word "Africa" conjures up pictures of us—prior to our disillusionment—and pictures of all sorts of wild animals. Well, we can wait for those. I will only name here that which remains in the memory of every one of Rommel's soldiers: Flies! Hundreds . . . thousands . . . indeed, billions . . . billions upon billions of flies. Will someone dare claim that they are not wild animals? Come on over here and let yourself be tortured by them. Then you will also come to believe that they are the wildest beings that live in God's animal kingdom. And you will no longer recognize yourselves in how you are turned wild by them. Frequently, you despair and want to capitulate, when you have smacked 500 dead, only to have another 1,000 swarm around you, taking their place. But self-preservation demands their constant destruction. For that reason, a soldier here without a fly swatter is as unthinkable as an explorer without a fur coat on the North Pole.

The other little animals here—such as scorpions, rats, field mice, jerboas, horned and sand vipers, yes, even tarantulas—don't do much to contributing to raise ones spirits. Before going to bed, you have to thoroughly search your tent every time; still, it is not infrequent that you find one of these little things in your boots. Nicer, but rare by contrast, at the desert hares and gazelles, but that names everything.

I do not want to close this chapter without saying a word about the technical situation. Due to a lack of experience, our technical preparations were completely insufficient. Just beyond Agedabia, that is, shortly after a few days of operations, the tanks started dying off in droves. Airborne dirt and sand put untold wear and tear on the engines; the local terrain ruined running gear and springs after the shortest of times. By the end of May, that is, after only eight weeks, some of us were already on our third engine. The motorcycles of the division are already completely worn out; the situation for the trucks is not much better. We only receive replacement parts in insufficient quantities. That we are able to roll out at all is exclusively thanks to the service of our drivers and maintenance personnel. They work tirelessly and almost continuously and perform unbelievable things. But who talks about them, especially the maintenance personnel. Who recognizes them out loud? Only the combat soldiers get awards. For that reason, their performance of duty is to be valued even more.

Canned sardines and Italian canned meat, hard tack and cheese in tubes were the main forms of nourishment for the German soldiers in the desert war.

I have to say it one more time: Our armored force is still very young and not everyone who commands in it has grown up with it. Understanding for the needs of a horse is far more widespread in our army than understanding for the needs of vehicles!

Despite all of the difficulties and disgusting things, the morale of our soldiers is unshakeable. Every new operation shakes off the lethargy coming from weeks of lying around and doing nothing and energizes them again to the old levels, allowing them to unfold their unique abilities.

The *DAK* produced a weekly newspaper for the soldiers. This is the 12 September 1941 issue of *Die Oase* ("The Oasis"). It was widely read by the troops. The lead-off headline reads that Leningrad has been encircled.

The 1st Company of the regiment during daily life in the desert. A dug-in tent and a dugout under the tank were "home" for weeks and months at a time for the tankers.

Summer 1941: During a period of relative calm, the forces in the field also found time for fun. In this case, the regiment held an "Arab festival."

The regimental band also provided music to soldiers in the field. The regimental band was directed by *Obermusikmeister* Albert Ott.

Finally, some soldiers were allowed to take home leave. Kuhn also wrote about that:[22]

The new rest area was near Marsa Luch. An old, shot-up wall that resembled a tower gave the locality its name. From there, we could be employ very quickly either at Tobruk or at Sollum. The watchword was to be ready to go at any time, but we had also been saved from the monotony of the endless, gray desert for a few weeks. We saw the green of a few palms and the changing colors of the sea and—we could jump in at any time! We had become so undemanding that we thought life at Marsa Luch was a paradise. July and August saw reorganization; overhauling of the materiel;

and training of the slowly arriving, completely untrained replacements. There was a lot to do, but there was also time for recreation, at least as far as that was possible under the dominant heat, the tormenting flies and the more than monotonous rations. Just the quiet alone proved our frazzled nerves with a necessary break. Only the English Air Force started to make its presence felt again; was it because it had received reinforcements or was it because our fighters had been weakened in favor of the Eastern Front? In any event, we were not spared bomber and fighter-bomber attacks there.

Who can describe our jubilation when home leave actually started to take place—who had even believed it despite the ever-increasing rumors?

22. Author's Note: Kuhn, 65.

The time between military operations was filled with intensive training of the personnel replacements.

Every unit was allowed to send 2% of its personnel. That meant one man a week for my company, assuming the first one from a group had returned after six weeks. Otherwise, the next group was not allowed to leave. In the best case, the last man in the company would be in line to go after 250 weeks, that is, in five years. On top of that, the six weeks were measured very tightly, if the man spent three weeks in Germany. But the mood meter rocketed skyward in an unimaginable way. The new regimental commander [*Oberstleutnant* Stephan], an old acquaintance from my time in Paderborn, arrived at the beginning of July. He did not show much understanding for the leave requests of officers. For that reason, no one dared to ask for it. But someone had to start, and since we had not liked one another that much since the first day we had met and I had little to risk, I had no reservations. In any event, I had

little hope that my request to get acquainted with my little boy would be approved. For that reason, my joy was all the greater when it was approved. Despite vigorous protests from the regimental physician, whom I had to see two days previously, I took charge of a transport of 30 leave takers from the division on 25 August. We took a vehicle to the airfield at Benina (near Bengasi), then an aircraft to Catania (Sicily) after intermediate landings in Sirte and Tripoli. From there, it was the train through Messina, Naples, Rome and Munich, with the result that we were in our home city of Berlin, lost and somewhat alienated, after only an eight-day trip on 1 September.

The "Africa Song" came into being in 1941. The lyrics to the song, which was based on the melody of *Lili Marleen* by Norbert Schultze, are seen on the following period postcard.

Tanks Are Rolling Forward in Africa

Lyrics by an unknown soldier;
music by Norbert Schultze

Across the Schelde, the Meuse and the Rhine
the tanks rolled into France.
The *Führer's* hussars in black garments;
that's how they assaulted and overran France.
The tracks rattle . . . the engine roars . . .
Tanks are rolling forward in Africa!
Tanks are rolling forward in Africa!

The sun glows hot over Africa's soil.
Our tank engines sing their song!
German tanks basking in the sun
Are ready for battle against England.
The tracks rattle . . . the engine roars . . .
Tanks are rolling forward in Africa!
Tanks are rolling forward in Africa!

Tanks of the *Führer*, watch out, you Britons!
They were conceived with you in mind!
They fear neither death nor the devil!
British haughtiness will shatter against them!
The tracks rattle . . . the engine roars . . .
Tanks are rolling forward in Africa!

Panzer rollen in Afrika vor

Worte von einem unbekannten Soldaten
Musik von Norbert Schultze

Ueber die Schelde, die Maas und den Rhein
stießen die Panzer nach Frankreich hinein.
Husaren des Führers im schwarzen Gewand,
so haben sie Frankreich im Sturm überrannt.
 Es rasseln die Ketten . . . es dröhnt der Motor . .
 Panzer rollen in Afrika vor!
 Panzer rollen in Afrika vor!

Heiß über Afrikas Boden die Sonne glüht.
Unsere Panzermotoren singen ihr Lied!
Deutsche Panzer im Sonnenbrand
stehen zur Schlacht gegen Engeland.
 Es rasseln die Ketten . . .
 Es dröhnt der Motör!
 Panzer rollen in Afrika vor!

Panzer des Führers, ihr Briten, habt acht!
Die sind zu eurer Vernichtung erdacht!
Sie fürchten vor Tod und vor Teufel sich nicht!
An ihnen der britische Hochmut zerbricht!
 Es rasseln die Ketten . . . es dröhnt der Motor . .
 Panzer rollen in Afrika vor!

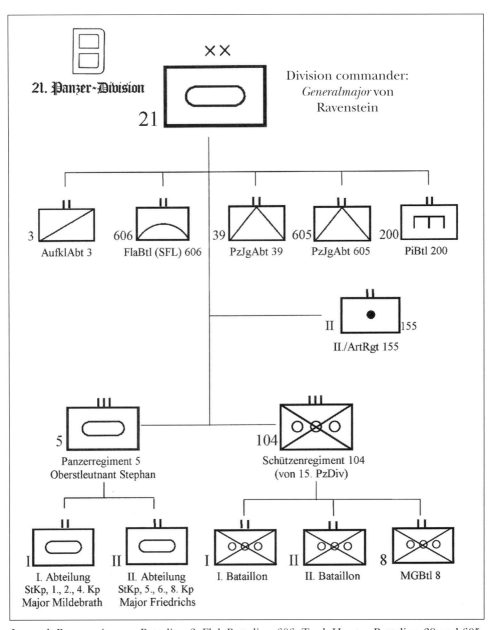

21. Panzer-Division

21

Division commander:
Generalmajor von
Ravenstein

3 AufklAbt 3

606 FlaBtl (SFL) 606

39 PzJgAbt 39

605 PzJgAbt 605

200 PiBtl 200

II **155** II./ArtRgt 155

5 Panzerregiment 5
Oberstleutnant Stephan

104 Schützenregiment 104
(von 15. PzDiv)

I I. Abteilung
StKp, 1., 2., 4. Kp
Major Mildebrath

II II. Abteilung
StKp, 5., 6., 8. Kp
Major Friedrichs

I I. Bataillon

II II. Bataillon

8 MGBtl 8

Legend: Reconnaissance Battalion 3, Flak Battalion 606, Tank Hunter Battalion 39 and 605, Engineer Battalion 200, 2nd Battalion Artillery Regiment 155, Panzer-Regiment 5, Rifle Regiment 104, Machine-Gun Battalion 8.

On 1 September, the division was redesignated and reorganized as the *21. Panzer-Division.*

Troop Elements of the *21. Panzer-Division*
(As of 1 November 1941)
(Minus command and logistics elements)[23]

In July 1941, the command and control structure of the Axis forces in Africa was changed. Rommel, who had been promoted to *General der Panzertruppen* after the Battle of Sollum, requested his forces be increased to at least four divisions, Malta be

eliminated as a threat and the convoys be protected better. But the offensive in the East that started on 21 June demanded all the forces Germany had, with the result that only the *Division z.b.V. Afrika*, which would later become the *90. leichte Division*, was formed.[24]

In addition, Rommel had recommended that the German and Italian forces at the front be formed into a *Panzergruppe,* an armored field army equivalent. That

23. Author's Note: Aberger, 79.

24. Translator's Note: *z.b.V. = zur besonderen Verwendung =* "for special purposes. Thus, the division was literally the Special-Purpose Division "Africa."

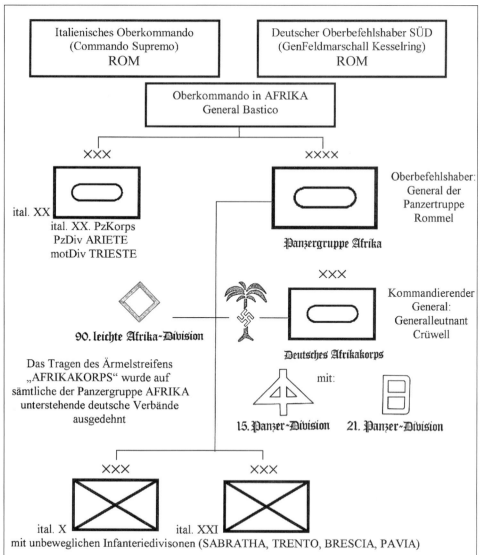

Italian Supreme Command
(*Commando Supremo*)
Rome

German Commander-in-Chief South
(*Generalfeldmarschall* Kesselring)
Rome

Supreme Command in Africa
General Bastico

Italian XX Armor Corps
Ariete Armored Division
Trieste Motorized Division

Panzergruppe Afrika
Commander-in-Chief
General der Panzertruppen
Rommel

Deutsches Afrika-Korps
Commanding General:
General Crüwell
With:
15. Panzer-Division
21. Panzer-Division

90. leichte-Division
The wear of the *Afrikakorps* cuff title was extended to all formations serving under *Panzergruppe Afrika*

Italian X Corps
Italian XXI Corps
With four static divisions
(*Sabratha, Trento, Brescia* and *Pavia*)

request was approved, and Rommel was designated the Commander-in-Chief of *Panzergruppe "Afrika"* on 8 July 1941. In the fall of 1941, the command structure of the Axis forces in North Africa is shown on the previous page.

During the time from July to October 1941, the air forces of both sides continued to remain active and made life difficult for the ground forces in the open terrain.

From 13 to 15 September, the *21. Panzer-Division* conducted *Operation "Sommernachtstraum"* (Operation "Summer Night's Dream"), which was intended to deliver a surprise attack against British logistics forces south of the Sollum Front. To that

end, the division was divided into three battle groups. Elements of the *15. Panzer-Division* formed one of the battle groups. Under the command of *Oberstleutnant* Stephan, it consisted of *Panzer-Regiment 5*, the *II./Artillerie-Regiment 155*, the *2./MG-Bataillon 8* and the *1./Pionier-Bataillon 200*. The operation was unsuccessful, since there were neither large-scale British combat forces in the vicinity of the border at the time nor the expected logistical elements and depots. After the offensive landed on open air, the attack formations were pulled back to their lines of departure. The *21. Panzer-Division* occupied assembly areas between the *Via Balbia* and the coast, 35 kilometers west of Bardia.

A *Panzer I* of the regiment tows a *Stuka* that had to make an emergency landing. Although the vehicle was no longer present on the official TO&E of the regiment (1 February 1941), it did not disappear from front-line troop duty until the fall of that year.

Operation "Sommernachtstraum" was not blessed with success. The advance hit empty space.

Panzer-Regiment 5 reported that between 30 March and 14 September 1941, it had destroyed or captured a total of 134 enemy armored vehicles, 2 armored cars, 30 antitank guns or self-propelled carriages, 33 field pieces and one aircraft.[25]

On 18 October, *Dr.* Selmayr was assigned to the regiment as a physician. The doctor, who became well respected and liked within the regiment, provided a firsthand account of his experiences:[26]

The billeting areas of the regiment were widely dispersed. As the result of danger from the air, the distance between each tent and each vehicle was about 100 meters. I was amazed; I could not find my way around. With somewhat mixed feelings, I reported to the regimental adjutant, *Oberleutnant* Böhm, whose billets were in a covered Horch staff car. The reception was cool. The regimental commander, *Oberstleutnant* Stephan, was not present; he was off hunting gazelle. I was directed to report in to the regimental physician, *Oberstabsarzt Dr.* Fregeneau. Fregeneau greeted me cordially. He was a doctor in Dar es Salem before the war; active duty; talked a lot about himself, but I liked him. He immediately briefed me on what was going on in the regiment. The regiment was very sick. All diarrhea, which had been treated with tannalbin up to that point. Fregeneau had been the first one to use the good microscopic equipment and determined amoebic dysentery. It was now being treated with yatren and rivanoletten.[27] He promised to bring me up to date with the microscopic diagnostics.

In addition to dysentery, there was also jaundice, diphtheria and wounds that "did not heal well." Even in the case of minor wounds, such as those that occur constantly occur from maintaining vehicles or from camel thorn bushes, developed lubricous scabs, but the wounds absolutely do not heal. Each of the physicians had their own methods for treating them, but nothing worked. At Fregeneau's suggestion, we cleaned the wounds and then placed a small piece of Prontosil bandage[28] on the wound, followed by plaster of Paris. But, as already said, all of the efforts were fruitless. The wounds healed best when there was opportunity to bathe in the sea, but that was only possible in an extremely small number of cases. As it turned cooler, the wounds healed; in my opinion, it was due to the disappearance of the flies; they reappeared when it turned warm.

Losses due to illness were very large; although the soldiers were supposed to remain with the forces in the field, if possible. Within the 2nd Battalion, a large tent was erected for those with diarrhea; where they received something akin to a diet. We had a rest home in Apolonia, where the people were sent to further recover their strength.

The old battalion surgeons had been killed or captured. The 1st Battalion had an *Assistenzarzt*, *Dr.* Stabich; the 2nd Battalion *Unterarzt Dr.* von Brunn. It was supposed to be decided the next day where I should be assigned, since another *Assistenzarzt*, *Dr.* Deutschländer, had also arrived. Spent the night with Stabich in the 1st Battalion. Well dug-in tent; nicely furnished. Food wasn't bad, but the coffee! Salt water! Ugh! Disgusting! We emptied my bottle; we also found some wine. Slept on a stretcher. Back to the regimental surgeon the next morning. The division still had not decided how I was to be employed. I was directed to remain here first and pull duty with the maintenance company.

Then I reported to *Oberstleutnant* Stephan. I climbed into a deeply dug-in tent and reported. Stephan, small, very lively, flyswatter in his hand,

---

25. Author's Note: Aberger, 77.

26. Author's Note: Selmayr, *Meine Erlebnisse im Weltkrieg 1939–1945*, 6 ff.

27. Translator's Note: Medical compounds often used in the treatment of tropical diseases.

28. Translator's Note: An antibacterial antibiotic that was first developed in Germany.

offered me a seat. "Take off your glasses!" I was wearing a pair of tinted glasses. "I want to look you in the eyes. Now tell me your life story!" I was somewhat trite to start out with, then I started to talk. After a short while, he interrupted me, told me one more time about my duty with the maintenance company and released me. A strange bird! Fregeneau, Stabich and I went to the division surgeon and then to the maintenance company. The acting commander was *Leutnant* Heimke, young, brash but very nice. He was happy that I had come and promised to have me picked up the following afternoon.

At the maintenance company I set up house in a truck from the 2nd Battalion that needed repairing. I set up after a fashion. The clearing station was in a small, round tent. Very meager, especially with regard to instruments and medicines. I muddled about, got my bearing and tried to adopt to my new surroundings.

Wherever I went, I noticed that I was a "newbie" in every respect and that the old "Africans" did not take me completely seriously.

Heimke was a terrific organizer. He lived feudally and even had a mess truck from captured spoils-of-war. The maintenance company knew how to take care of itself. I soon developed good camaraderie with him and his right-hand man, *Leutnant* Trautvetter. During the evenings, we often sat and played cards, sipping a container of water from Derna.

The typical day in the maintenance company: First call at 0600 hours. I didn't allow myself to be bothered and continued to doze. At 0700 hours, my batman, Braun, brought me coffee. Drunk hot, it was still drinkable, but the salt taste was nauseating. The wells on hand were no longer up to the task, with the result that they only yielded brackish water. Along with the coffee was army bread and bitter marmalade. I did my morning wash-up and then the usual trip with the shovel. Of course, my stool was also

quite thin, but I still felt pretty good. At 0900 hours, there was sick call. Usually around 10 sick soldiers, everything very primitive. I didn't care for the medical NCO. Sent a man to the dentist yesterday to get a tooth extracted, but he came back today, since he needed permission from the company commander, in accordance with a regimental directive. I was enraged that there was that sort of interference [in medical affairs]. Heimke confirmed the man's statement but immediately agreed that only my directives would be in force. Had a telephonic run-in with a medical NCO, Werner, from the 2nd Battalion, since an ambulance to evacuate a man sick with diphtheria took forever to arrive.

After sick call, gamboled over to Heimke; lunch in my vehicle. Bread with *AM*, a tough, fatty beef with lots of chucks of fat or canned sardines or tubed cheese, a soft cheese with ill-defined taste. After a noon nap, reading from books from the troop library or books about tropical diseases. At 1700 hours, dinner with all the officers and shop foremen, etc. Dinner varies; get reasonably full. Afterwards, a little chatting with Heimke. As it turned dark, parachute flares and bombs fell on the *Via Balbia* about 3 kilometers away. About 2200 hours I went to bed.

There was a small officer social in the 4th Company; a little drunkenness. I still don't feel quite comfortable with everyone. Last officer call before the regiment departs. Led by *Major* Mildebrath: *Herr* Scorm—the leader of the rear detachment—enemy tanks are approaching you from the east, west and south, and the sea is to the north: What are your orders?"

"*Herr Major*, I'd summon the regimental bandmaster and order him to play 'Enemy all around us!'" General laughter all around, but Mildebrath did not appear pleased. There was supposed to be another get-together on 9 November, but it was cancelled because the lights didn't work . . .

Sick call in the desert. This photo was taken somewhere in the *15. Panzer-Division* and shows a battalion physician, *Dr.* Unverzagt, giving immunization shots.

6. 18 November to the End of December 1941: Winter Fighting (British Operation "Crusader")

The English used the time of relative quiet between July and November 1941 to considerably reinforce their forces in North Africa. That was possible by moving around the Cape of Good Hope as far as the Nile. All of the forces were assembled into the newly formed 8th Army, which had approximately 800 tanks—including some 300 Lend-Lease Stuart light tanks from the USA—1,000 artillery pieces and 34,000 trucks. In November, the Royal Air Force had some 550 aircraft on its rosters. The English wanted to launch another offensive in 1941 with those forces. The planned operation received the codename of "Crusader."

For the Axis forces, the question of logistics remained a primary concern for the conduct of war. Only about half of the sea transports made it, with the result that only a portion of the daily needs of some 1,500 tones of logistics reached the forces at the front. Supplies trickled; they did not flow. *Panzergruppe Afrika* had 182 *Panzer III's* and *IV's* in the middle of November. The *Luftwaffe* had a total of 280 operational aircraft.

The German forces were aware that the British forces were being constantly reinforced. Rommel intended to take the beleaguered garrison of Tobruk before the British launched their offensive, so as to free up the siege forces for employment along the Libyan-Egyptian border. It was intended to employ the *15. Panzer-Division* and the *90. leichte Division* for the assault on Tobruk, scheduled for 20 November. The *21. Panzer-Division* and the Italian forces were intended to defend against any possible British offensive efforts from the east and south during the intended offensive, code-named *Operation "Hochwasser"* (Operation "Flood"). The latter forces occupied their assembly areas by 16 November.

The African winter commenced with rain showers and cold sandstorms. On 17 November, for the first time in 60 years, there was a cloudburst over the desert. The *wadis*, which had been dried up, filled and actually flooded.

17 November 1941: Cloudburst in the desert.

Under the cover of the weather conditions, the British completed their approach march for their operation. On the morning of 18 November, the British launched their offensive with a strong reconnaissance-in-force along a broad front with some 1,000 tanks and 100,000 soldiers. The objective was to take Cyrenaica and advance on Tripoli. The lead attack elements took Gabr Saleh on 18 November. The German security forces along the border—*Aufklärungs-Abteilung 3 (mot)* and *Aufklärungs-Abteilung 33 (mot)*—pulled back. The British continued their offensive on 19 November in the direction of Sidi Azeiz, Sidi Rezegh and Bir el Gobi. It was at that point that the headquarters of *Panzergruppe Afrika* recognized that the British had launched their actual offensive, after it had initially been assumed to just be a reconnaissance-in-force. Rommel dropped his plans to take Tobruk.

During the afternoon of 19 November, the reinforced *Panzer-Regiment 5*, with 120 operational tanks, encountered strong enemy forces northeast of Gabr Saleh as it advanced as the armored battle group of the *21. Panzer-Division*. By that evening, the

British were forced back, having lost 23 Stuarts to the Germans' 3 tanks. The *Ariete* Armored Division held its positions at Bir el Gobi.

So as to avoid dissipating its strength, the Commanding general of the *DAK*, *Generalleutnant* Crüwell, recommended that the identified enemy forces be attacked in succession. An attack was initially conducted on 20 November by both the *15. Panzer-Division* and the *21. Panzer-Division* in the direction of Sidi Omar. Towards the evening of the same day, the attack was called off because a critical situation had developed in the Sidi Rezegh area in the meantime. It was there that the British had launched their main effort.

During the night of 20–21 November, the *DAK* disengaged from the enemy and moved northwest. General Auchinleck, the British Commander-in-Chief, ordered the Tobruk garrison to break out towards El Duda on 21 November. It was intended for the British 7th Armoured Division to launch a relief effort from the direction of Sidi Rezegh. The Tobruk breakout to the southeast led to a penetration that was deep and some 3.5 kilometers wide, but it was

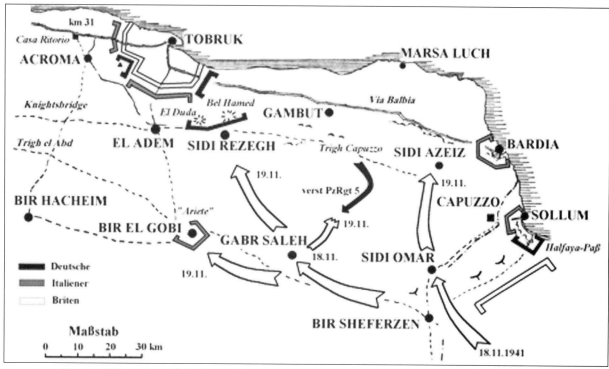

18 and 19 November 1941: Start of Operation "Crusader." Attack by the British on a broad front.

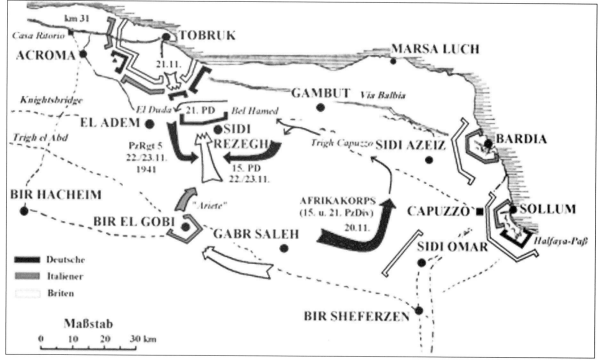

20 to 23 November 1941: "Crusader" develops.

not able to completely break through. The attack by the 7th Armoured Division from the south bogged down along the edge of the El Duda–Bel Hamed mountain range.

On 22 November, the British encircled the German forces around Sollum. The next day, *Totensonntag*,[29] has entered the history books as a memorable day for the fighting in North Africa. The *21. Panzer-Division*, minus *Panzer-Regiment 5*, fixed the enemy forces to its front along the mountain range to either side of Sidi Rezegh. That same morning, *Panzer-Regiment 5* attacked the British forces from the west, while the *15. Panzer-Division* attacked from the east. The *Ariete* attacked from the south to land in the enemy's rear.

The *15. Panzer-Division* fought its way through a defensive sector measuring 8 kilometers wide and 10 kilometers deep; *Panzer-Regiment 5* knocked out 32 enemy tanks, 18 antitank guns and 3 batteries of artillery. In all, 2,000 prisoners were taken. Only

portions of the enemy force were able to escape to the southeast. The Armed forces Daily Report of 23 November announced:[30]

> In North Africa, the German-Italian forces successfully engaged and destroyed more than 260 tanks and about 200 armored vehicles of the British forces that had advanced from the southeast . . . The fighting in North Africa continues with heavy fighting.

By the evening of 23 November, *Panzer-Regiment 5* had only 32 operational tanks left; *Panzer-Regiment 8* of the *15. Panzer-Division* had only 61. In all, the *DAK* had lost 72 tanks in the fighting.[31] While the Germans had no tank reserves, the British held back some 200 tanks in the area around Gabr Saleh.

Despite his numerical superiority, Rommel decided during the night of 23–24 November to advance in the direction of the Libyan-Egyptian frontier with a battle group. It was intended for the

---

29. Translator's Note: "Sunday of the dead." Traditionally, the Sunday before the first Advent is set aside to commemorate the dead.

30. Author's Note: Köhler, 48.

31. Author's Note: Aberger, 96.

Top: 23 November 1941: The Fighting on *Totensonntag*. The battlefield at Sidi Rezegh.

DAK to cut off the 8th Army from its rearward lines of communications and then eliminate the enemy forces in the area around Sollum. Rommel left his headquarters and accompanied the lead attack elements in his captured English armored car, a "Mammoth."

The two German armored divisions advanced in the direction of Sidi Omar, followed by the *Ariete*. *Panzer-Regiment 5* became engaged in a firefight with enemy tanks north of Gabr Saleh on 24 November; it was initially fixed in place there. The remaining elements of the division reached the border fence around 1600 hours and advanced from there at a fast clip, swinging east in the direction of Halfaya Pass. By the time it turned dark, the division was strung out about 70 kilometers. The *15. Panzer-Division* had its forces in the Sidi Omar area that evening. The *Ariete* was held up and did not close with the German divisions.

On 25 November, the *15. Panzer-Division* advanced on a 30-kilometer-wide front between Sidi Azeiz and Sidi Omar to the east, while the *21. Panzer-Division* had difficulty in assembling the forces

that had spread out so far the previous day. In the meantime, *Panzer-Regiment 5* had disengaged from the enemy forces at Gabr Saleh, but it marched too far to the south with its 21 operational tanks in its effort to close up with it parent division. After the regiment discovered its error and swung to the north, the regimental commander, *Oberstleutnant* Stephan, was killed in an air attack.[32]

Major Mildebrath, the commander of the 1st battalion, was entrusted with acting command of the regiment. The regiment then encountered a belt of antitank guns and mines around Sidi Omar that could not be penetrated. In the course of that fighting, the regiment lost 15 tanks, with the result that it only had 13 operational ones left. Radio contact was then lost between the acting regimental commander's vehicle and the two battalions. As a result, the 1st Battalion continued too far to the south, and the 2nd Battalion too far to the west. It was not until 27 November that the two formations could rejoin.

32. Author's Note: Aberger, 101.

Knocked-out British
Stuart light tanks.

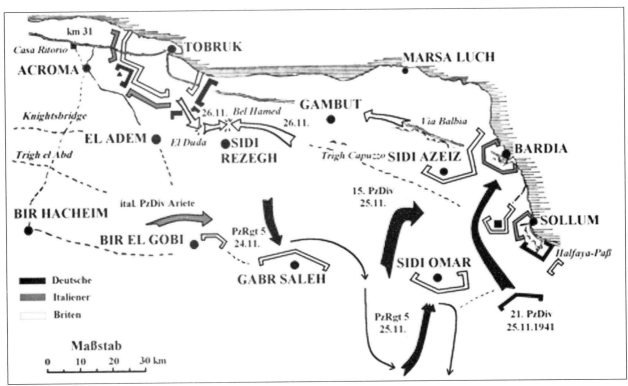

24 to 26 November 1941: The fighting continues.

In the meantime, the situation around Tobruk had taken a dramatic turn for the worse. The enemy's bridgehead had been expanded, and a New Zealand division attacking from the east had taken the high ground between El Duda and Bel Hamed. During the afternoon of 26 November, the two attack forces established contact. As opposed to the assumption made by the German command, the enemy had not been beaten; indeed, after the introduction of reserves, he had resumed the initiative.

The operations officer of *Panzergruppe Afrika*, *Oberstleutnant* Westphal, had not had any contact from the command post with Rommel for days. The Commander-in-Chief was with the forces involved in the seesaw fighting around Sollum. When all efforts to reach Rommel had failed, Westphal acted on his own initiative. On 26 November, he issued the following radio order to the forces in the field in light of the critical situation around Tobruk: "Under rescission of all previous orders, the *DAK* is to move in the direction of Tobruk as rapidly as possible."

On 27 November, the *DAK* started moving west from the Sollum Front towards Tobruk. On 29 November, the commander of the *21. Panzer-Division*, *Generalmajor* von Ravenstein, was captured by the British as the result of unfortunate circumstances. *Generalmajor* Böttcher assumed acting command.

As a result of the attacks, advances and withdrawal movements of the fighting, there was considerable confusion among the troop elements of both sides on the battlefield. Inadequate radio communications on the German side made command and control exceptionally difficult. Planned operations dissolved into a series of local engagements, which cannot be portrayed here in their entirety due to their number.

Knocked-out English Crusader II tank in November 1941.

On 3 December, the two tank regiments of the *DAK* had only 34 operational tanks, representing only 13% of their authorized strengths. More than 20% of the tanks were in repair. During the recent round of winter fighting, 167 tanks were completely written off.[33]

The other combat arms—artillery, *Flak*, engineers and antitank elements—had only about 50% of their authorized strengths. The logistical troops had also suffered considerable casualties. Particularly disadvantageous was the air superiority of the Royal Air Force and the missing air support on the German side. The Axis forces could not count on any reinforcements before January 1942. The British forces, on the other hand, were able to make up their losses—which had been considerable, numbering some 800 tanks—through their extensive reserves.

The time up to 6 December was marked mostly by reassembling and reorganizing the force. The ring around Tobruk was temporarily closed again. An effort was also made—in vain—to destroy enemy formations in the Bir el Gobi and Gabr Saleh areas.

Rommel recognized that it was no longer possible to maintain the siege of Tobruk, thanks to the British attacks in the El Adem area. In addition, due to the large friendly losses, it was no longer possible to decisively defeat the enemy. Despite considerable success, the Axis forces were unable to turn the tide in favor of the Axis as a result of the winter fighting around Sollum and Tobruk. Based on the situation, it was becoming imperative to prevent *Panzergruppe Afrika* from being destroyed. That meant the abandonment of terrain in order to

33. Author's Note: Kühn, 86.

pull back to terrain that was particularly well suited for the defense and to wait there until such time as new forces could be introduced for a counterattack.

When the danger of being encircled by the enemy from the south started to demonstrate itself, Rommel ordered the withdrawal of *Panzergruppe Afrika* on 7 December. It was to move initially to the Gazala Position. That ended the encirclement of Tobruk.

At that point, it was imperative to secure the withdrawal of the non-motorized forces—especially the Italian infantry divisions, which were not motorized at all—the artillery and the logistics forces. The three German divisions were still strong enough to ensure that. The German command saw its most important mission in preventing the British 8th Army from advancing rapidly through Cyrenaica to the eastern edge of the Sirte Bend.

On 6 December, *Panzer-Regiment 5* had 4 *Panzer II's*, 10 *Panzer III's*, 5 *Panzer IV's* and 1 *Panzer-befehlswagen III*.

Repairing damaged running gear on a *Panzer III*.

The abandonment of the front around Tobruk also meant the simultaneous loss of the strongpoints around Sollum. Bardia was able to hold out until 2 January 1942; Halfaya Pass until 17 January. For every day that the brave defenders of Halfaya Pass held out, the English were deprived usage of the coastal road, thus requiring the movement of logistics in a time-consuming and laborious fashion through the desert.

For the Axis forces, the logistical lines of communication were shortened, which allowed *Panzergruppe Afrika* to supply its elements with sufficient fuel and ammunition from the depots in Tmimi. During the retreat, the formations were able to bring back valuable non-consumables with them to the west.

Enemy penetrations into the Gazala Position were cleaned up by the combined efforts of the two tank regiments. During the night of 16–17 December, the *DAK* was able to disengage unnoticed from the enemy out of the Gazala Position and moved 75 kilometers farther west to the area around Mechili, where it established new delaying positions. *Stuka* attacks on enemy forces attacking to the front brought about effective relief.

The danger of an envelopment from the south started to surface. If the enemy succeeded in taking the area around Agedabia, then the Axis forces in northern Cyrenaica would be cut off. As a result, the positions around Mechili were evacuated and the withdrawal west continued.

It was intended to transport the two remaining missing companies of *Panzer-Regiment 5*—the 3rd and 7th Companies—on 13 and 19 December. But the transport ships with 11 *Panzer II's* and 34 *Panzer III's* were sunk.[34]

On 20 December, the *DAK* reached the area around Bengasi. A member of the force at the time wrote of the experience:[35]

A radio message reached us that the depots in Bengasi had been opened to all. Vehicles from all units, inasmuch as their commanders allowed them, took off. Things were loaded, loaded to the seams: Canned meat, butter, cans of fish, cans of fruit and vegetables, chocolate and cigarettes. There were even sacks of sugar and noodles there. In one area, we found fresh meat and—a rarity—potatoes. Some idle gossipers claimed that some vehicles had shaving cream and toothpaste on board that was enough to last for years. The number of Italians, both in uniform and civilian clothes, and Arabs streaming into the depots grew ever larger.

Wild plundering started. Many carted off so much that they almost collapsed under the load and had to throw away some things after a few hundred meters.

There was mad confusion on the *Via Balbia*. Italian trucks and armored vehicles, soldiers hanging off, pushed their way between vehicles that were loaded with Italian men, women and children, with household goods piled high. Why the settlers were fleeing was not exactly clear. A British garrison had already been there without doing them any harm. Who would provide them with fuel, rations and water on the long road to Tripoli? Probably the combat forces. You couldn't leave those people to their fate. They were especially endangered during aerial attacks. Soldiers had learned to quickly take cover; but mothers with small children? The pilot, who was attacking a column, probably could not differentiate between military and civilian vehicles.

The *21. Panzer-Division* occupied defensive positions east of Beda Fomm on 23 December. The delaying action there was of decisive importance for the evacuation of the important supply depots in Bengasi. The *DAK* then marched on 25 December to an area

34. Author's Note: Jentz, 174.

35. Author's Note: Aberger, 132 ff.

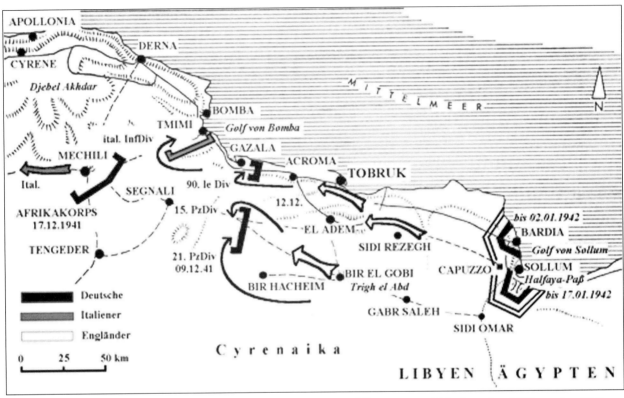

Abandonment of the Tobruk Front and Withdrawal Movements of *Panzergruppe Afrika* from 9 to 17 December 1941.

15 kilometers southwest of Agedabia, the wheeled elements on the *Via Balbia,* the tracked elements to the south. The new positions were intended to screen the right flank of the field army.

On 26 December, the *DAK* interdicted a thrust towards the *Via Balbia.* On 28 and 29 December, it attacked the British 22nd Armoured brigade at Haseiat, which was attempting to envelop from the south and advance on the *Via Balbia.* A large number of enemy vehicles were destroyed during the engagement with few friendly losses.

The *DAK* spent the last day of the year in an assembly area in the high ground of Belaudah, 20 kilometers southeast of Agedabia. When Operation "Crusader" started on 18 November, *Panzer-Regiment 5* had had 124 operational tanks. On 31 December,

only eight were reported as operational. During the fighting during the winter, the regiment knocked out or captured 161 enemy tanks and 15 armored cars. It had also eliminated 42 antitank guns and self-propelled guns, as well as 37 towed artillery pieces. Several hundred prisoners had been taken; vehicles of all types had been captured.[36]

---

36. Author's Note: *Major* Mildebrath, After-Action Report of the *Panzer-Regiment 5* from 17 November to 31 December 1941.

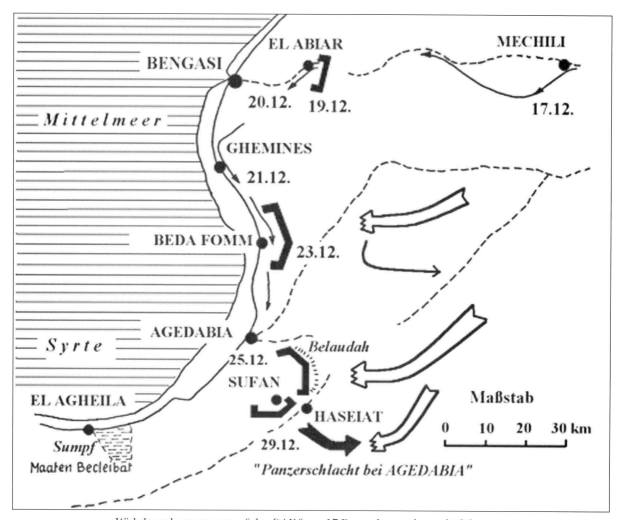

Withdrawal movements of the *DAK* from 17 December to the end of the year.

7. Logistics in Africa, 1941

Supplies

The forces in North Africa were more dependent on supplies than in Europe, since there was no "self-help." Supply was also dependent upon its transport across the Mediterranean or through the *Luftwaffe*. A portion of the trucks available for supply could not be used in the desert and restricted to the few improved roads (e.g., *Via Balbia*). To relieve the road traffic somewhat, a very limited coastal transport network was established. In the vicinity of the front, there were no harbors of note, only simple landing docks. The fuel consumption rates, which had been based on European scenarios, turned out to be significantly higher in the tropical climate. In addition, higher consumption of coolant water and lubricants had to be taken into account. The road and terrain conditions shortened the usual life of tires considerably. Portions of the supply columns had to be employed exclusively for the transport of water. Due to the short water supply, the following was rationed: 5 liters a day for each man; 20 liters of coolant water every two days for armored vehicles and trucks (one fuel can); 40 liters of coolant water for each tank every two days.[37]

As the result of a ban on the transport of mail, it was reported on 25 May, that 100 tons of field post was warehoused in Naples. The field army requested the mail be air-transported to derma, where it was then sent forward on available space on supply columns.

Starting in the middle of August, navy soap was issued in addition to the army soap. Since it was soluble in salt water, it was well suited for washing clothes in the desert.

Despite that, personal hygiene and the cleaning of clothes remained a problem. There was seldom sufficient water for that purpose and the issued potable water was barely enough to satisfy thirst on hot days.

There were shortages of tank, artillery, antitank and *Flak* ammunition.

The supply columns often had difficulties finding the combat forces they were supporting and were often exposed to attacks from the air and from armored car patrols.

The forces in the field were able to cover many of their needs for rations and fuel by using captured stocks.

37. Author's Note: Aberger, 143.

Vehicle Repair

Wear and tear on vehicles was very high. Approximately 40% of the vehicle fleet was undergoing repair at any given time. As a result of the inadequate supply of spare and replacement parts, vehicles were in a non-operational status for long periods.

The maintenance services earned special praise for their efforts in attempting to recover and repair combat vehicles, on the battlefield, if possible. When the combat forces had to give up terrain and the maintenance companies also had to move as a result, many damaged and non-mobile tanks had to be left behind because there was not sufficient recovery capacity.

Medical Services

During the first few months of 1941, approximately 70% of the medical supplies sent to Africa were sunk. Although medicines and dressing materials could be sent by air, there was still a considerable lack of stretchers, operation room equipment, tents, beds, etc.[38]

The monotonous nutrition and the complete lack of fresh fruit and vegetables led to a rapid decline in strength on the part of the soldiers and a

38. Author's Note: Aberger, 155.

An incapacitated *Panzer III* is loaded on a tank transporter for delivery to a maintenance unit.

susceptibility to diseases. There were high numbers of sick due to flesh wounds that did not heal properly, stomach and kidney infections and some cases of jaundice. The losses due to sickness exceeded those due to wounds considerably. In September, 11,000 sick personnel were reported, 25% of the forces in the field.

Pay

Based on an agreement with the Italian government, the German soldiers employed in Libya were supposed to get tropical supplemental pay. The Germans believed this should be the same for all ranks, but that did not sit well with the pronounced class system of the Italians, which dictated a sharp distinction between the differing rank groups. This was expressed not only in the differing quality of the uniforms, but also in the rations. For the Germans, rations were distributed equally, regardless of rank. The Italians structured the supplemental pay based on their viewpoint. Enlisted personnel received a supplement of 2 *Reichsmark* daily, noncommissioned officers 3 *Reichsmark* and officers 4 *Reichsmark*. The aggregated amount was paid out upon leaving Africa.

8. Evaluation of the Campaign in Africa, 1941

In 1941, Germany had no interest in a campaign in North Africa. The German Armed Forces were fully committed in Europe. The defeats suffered by the Italian allies in Libya and the political and military consequences—growing ever more disadvantageous and weighty—forced Germany to help the Italians.

The contingents sent to the North African theater in 1941—initially two, then three divisions—proved insufficient to meet the requirements of a campaign on another continent against a force, numerically vastly superior in both numbers and combat power. Although North Africa was the main theater of war for the Italians, the burden of fighting increasingly fell to the Germans, for whom Africa was a secondary theater. Much was expected, but little was given in support.

The operations of *Panzergruppe Afrika* were marked by the effort to employ its numerically inferior forces in an offensive manner and with its main effort at decisive locations. If there were to be any success at all for the Axis forces, then it could only be brought about by offensive operations. Persisting in the defensive would have unavoidably led to the loss of North Africa for the Axis, even as early as

Water cans, indicated by the white crosses, are filled at a water point.

1941. Even the defense was conducted aggressively by Rommel and his commanders, keeping their forces mobile and attacking whenever possible. The possession of terrain played a subordinate role.

The German soldiers in Africa had to improvise to a great extent. Their achievements deserve respect, since they had absolutely no colonial experience.

With some exceptions, the desert offered ideal terrain for motorized and armored forces, which could bring their ability to maneuver and fire to bear without restriction. Tanks, armored cars, 8.8-centimeter *Flak* and wide-ranging artillery were the ideal weapons systems for the desert. The Italian infantry divisions, on the other hand, possessed little combat value; indeed, they could even be considered somewhat of a hindrance, as was demonstrated during the withdrawal movements of November and December.

During the winter fighting of 1941, the German forces scored a considerable success against the British formations by destroying 814 armored vehicles of all types. Since no reinforcements were forthcoming, however, they proved to be too weak in the end to decide the fighting in their favor. Rommel was able to get his way in withdrawing from the Tobruk Front at the end of 1941 all the way to the border of Tripolitania—abandoning Cyrenaica along the way—against the desires of his superiors. The course of the final fighting of the year made it necessary to conduct a large-scale withdrawal all the way to the Sirte Bend, since only the surrender of Cyrenaica would allow him to retain forces for a later counterattack.

The armored forces of the *DAK*—*Panzer-Regiment 5* of the *21. Panzer-Division* and *Panzer-Regiment 8* of the *15. Panzer-Division*—played a key role in the combined arms fight. Their losses in tanks were correspondingly high.

As a result, *Panzer-Regiment 5* end 1941 with only 8 operational tanks, which represented only 4% of its authorized strength of 206 tanks (based on eight companies and the TO&E of 1 February 1941).

9. Overview of *Panzer-Regiment 5* in the Campaign in North Africa in 1941

13 October 1940	*Oberst* Olbrich assumes command of the regiment
10 March 1941	The regiment unloads in the harbor of Tripoli
13–30 March	Defensive positions established west of El Agheila
31 March–7 April	Tobruk is encircled, attacks on the fortress and capture of the *Ras el Madauer*
15–17 June	Armored engagement at Sollum; British Operation "Battleaxe"
1 July	*Oberstleutnant* Stephan assumes command of the regiment
13–15 September	Reconnaissance-in-force in the direction of the Egyptian border; *Operation "Sommernachtstraum"*
18 November	Start of the fighting in the Marmarica; British Operation "Crusader" (18 November to 17 December 1941)
23 November	Fighting on *Totensonntag* at Sidi Rezegh
25 November	*Oberstleutnant* Stephan killed at Sidi Omar; *Major* Mildebrath assumes acting command of the regiment
27 November–7 December	Attacks in the Tobruk area; Fighting for Bir el Gobi
8–17 December	Withdrawal to the Gazala Position; mobile defense
18–31 December	Withdrawal from Cyrenaica; mobile defense south of Bengasi; armored engagement at Agedabia (28–29 December 1941)
31 December	Regiment in an assembly area southeast of Agedabia

"Christmas Greetings from Africa." A postcard printed for members of the *DAK* in Libya in 1941.

A German cemetery in Cyrenaica.

"Africa" ring, as worn by *Oberleutnant* Sandrock, a company commander. It was purchased from a silversmith in the Arab quarter of Tripoli in 1941.

A *Panzerbefehlswagen I* of the regiment passes the sign for the entrance to Tripoli. Note the water cans on the rear deck of the vehicle.

A *Panzer I* of the regimental headquarters is painted in desert camouflage sand (*sandgelb*) from its original dark gray (*panzergrau*).

Panzer II's of the regiment, transported by "lowboy" trailers, roll through the *Arco dei Fileni*, the Italian victory arch on the border between Tripolitania and Libya.

German and Italian comrades-in-arms pose beside a *Panzer III*. Note the protective coverings placed over the main gun and the coaxial machine gun and the stowage of canteens on the outside of the turret.

The regiment heads towards the front on the *Via Balbia*, passing light Italian tankettes, referred to by the German tankers as "cookie tins."

The desert after the coastal road was left. *Panzer III's* of the regiment advance in the direction of Cyrenaica.

2 April 1941: The regiment undergoes its baptism of fire in the desert. The tank fighting at Agedabia. This photograph was taken through a vision port.

Under enemy fire.

2 April 1941, Agedabia: A knocked-out Mark II.

This Mark II "Matilda" sustained hits on its turret race, side, front and mantlet.

The first British prisioners

Soldiers of the regiment take a look at an Italian M13/40 medium tank.

The advance continues.

The *Panzerbefehlswagen III* of the regimental commander. The attack starts up.

8 April 1941: Tankers of the regiment after the taking of Derna.

The *Panzer I* was still in service with the regiment in 1941.

Wheeled vehicles of the regiment in Derna.

This *Panzer II* of the regimental headquarters has sustained a hit in the side. Note that the tanker inspecting the damage is wearing the *Panzer* beret without the crash helmet and not the iconic billed tropical field cap so often associated with the *DAK*.

9 April 1941 in the Derna-Tmimi area: The attack on Tobruk is continued.

United in death: Graves of both German and Commonwealth soldiers in the spring of 1941 at El Adem.

Gazala was taken on 9 April 1941 and Rommel's forces were at the gates of Tobruk the next day. A palm tree with a superimposed swastika became the identifying insignia of the *DAK*.

Outside of Tobruk in April 1941: To the right in the picture is *Leutnant* Gerd Frank-Lindheim of the 6th Company of the regiment. He wears a rubberized overcoat that was originally intended for motorcycle dispatch riders. The officer to his right wears the standard wool tropical overcoat.

A *Panzer IV*, Model D, of the 8th Company outside of Tobruk. It is the platoon leader's vehicle of the 1st Platoon (*811*).

During the siege of Tobruk, the Italians built a bypass road around the fortress.

At the end of May, tanks of the regiment assemble prior to the launch of *Operation "Skorpion,"* the effort to retake Halfaya Pass.

A British A 9 Cruiser tank knocked out by the 6th Company.

Knocked-out British tankettes.

Providing a wounded soldier with water. The wounded man wears British tanker coveralls and a German overseas cap, which meant he was undoubtedly a German soldier wearing captured stocks.

Key terrain during the fighting for Sollum: Lower Sollum and Halfaya Pass.

5–17 June 1941: The armored engagement at Sollum. Knocked-out British 2-pounder antitank gun mounted on a truck.

Burned-out
Panzer III.

Generalleutnant Rommel during the Sollum fighting.

The British suffered considerably more tank losses. A Crusader complete with anachronistic machine-gun turret.

A Mark II captured by the regiment at Sollum. The British driver, seen on the front slope of the tank, seems to enjoy posing with his captors.

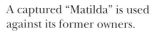

A captured "Matilda" is used against its former owners.

Rommel, who was promoted to *General der Panzertruppen* after the fighting at Sollum, is seen presenting deserving soldiers of the regiment with awards.

German and Italian military cemetery in Bardia after the summer fighting of 1941.

Soldiers of the regiment inspect a dud from a British 38-centimeter coastal artillery gun.

A *Panzer III* of the regimental headquarters performs coastal security in the vicinity of Marsa Luch.

The crew of a *Panzer III* tries to make it as cozy as possible in the assembly area around Marsa Luch.

The forces in the field take it easy after the hard campaigning of the previous few months.

Life in the desert was hard for soldiers of both sides. For the German soldier, it was marked by constant shortages. Improvisation and imagination were in high demand.

Rations issue: given the monotonous food provided, not as popular as it should have been.

A guard post is dug out.

An "air raid bunker" has been dug under this halftrack prime mover. The dugout probably served as quarters for the vehicle's crew.

A "whore's bath" in the desert.

August Klostermann of the 1st Company washes uniform articles with fuel.

A field barber shop.

The rear deck of a tank was never the most comfortable place to sleep.

Tankers of the 4th Company enjoy some time off.

Radio-operator training.

The assembly area of the 2nd Battalion in the Marsa Luch area.

Commanders' call in the 2nd Battalion.

Following the meeting, the regimental band provides a little music.

Men of the 5th Tank of the 1st Platoon of the 6th Company a smoke break.

Oberleutnant Werner Grün in June 1941 as the company commander of the 6th Company. He was decorated with the Knight's Cross to the Iron Cross on 8 February 1943 as a *Hauptmann* and acting commander of the 1st Battalion of the regiment, marking him as the ninth and last recipient of the high award within the regiment.

The command post and company area of the 6th Company.

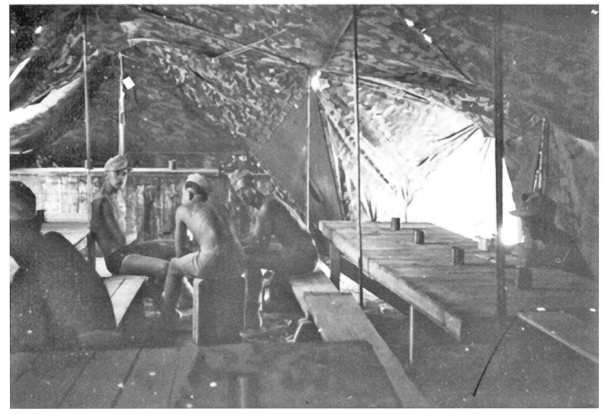

Inside the command post and company area.

A game of chess on a *Panzer III*. Note the bleached-out appearance of the caps on the soldiers. This was sometimes artificially induced by exposing the caps to gas training aids in an enclosed area.

Chess seems to have been a popular pastime in the 6th Company.

An "Arab" fest held by the regiment in the Marsa Luch assembly area.

The regiment maintained a soldiers' home in Appolonia to the west of Derna. It was named after the regimental commander of the time, *Oberstleutnant* Stephan.

"Derna water" has arrived. The signals officer of the 2nd Battalion, *Leutnant* Rudolf Wendorff, has provided information concerning water in the desert:

I should mention that we did not have any normal drinking water at Marsa Luch . . . instead, it was only salt water. That was a new and unpleasant experience, which I often reflect on. Located between the Mediterranean and the so-called coastal road, there was no normal water; instead there were a few wells with water that had salt in it, which we had to get used to.

We always received tea to drink, but it was this salt tea with a somewhat terrible taste—for weeks and months on end! Health wise, it most certainly did us no damage, but drinking became a true exercise of duty.

Once a week, we receive normal salt-free water for our tea and for us personally. That was a day of celebration. *Feldwebel* Jüptner, the head of the water column, came from the neighboring city of Derna, where he tanked up specially marked water cans with white crosses with "potable water" from a well that met military standards.

Whenever the truck with this water appeared, there was a hue and cry throughout the battalion that spread across the broad terrain: "Derna water! . . . Derna water!"

Cakes are baked for a special
occasion within the 6th Company.

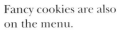

Fancy cookies are also
on the menu.

An *MG 34* mounted on a tripod
for air defense.

Late in the summer of 1941: Personnel and materiel replacements for the regiment on the Italian transporter *Neptunia* during the crossing of the Mediterranean.

November 1941: *Oberleutnant* Hans Sandrock (third from the viewer's right) and his crew. Sandrock was the company commander of the 1st Company and received the Knight's Cross to the Iron Cross on 18 October 1941.

17 November 1941: The winter in Africa arrived with rain showers and cold sand storms. For the first time in 60 years, there were cloudbursts over the desert. The *wadis* flooded.

The winter fighting of 1941 started with flooding in the desert.

Werner Fleck, a gunner in the 1st Company (*131*), looks for his belongings in the flooded tent area.

A impromptu river-crossing operation in the desert!

Waiting for the order to attack. *Panzer III* number *131* is the vehicle of the platoon leader, *Leutnant* Stein.

Situation briefing at the division command half-track.

Oberstleutnant Stephan, on the viewer's left, in consultation with the commander of the *15. Panzer-Division, Generalmajor* Neumann-Silkow. Stephan was killed during an air attack on 25 November 1941.

23 November 1941: The regiment fights on *Totensonntag* in the Sidi Rezegh area.

British soldiers surrender.

Rommel, on the viewer's left, accompanied the attack of the 2nd Battalion. He has donned a tropical field billed cap in lieu of his more typical visor cap.

November 1941: The *Panzerbefehlswagen III* of *Hauptmann* Gierga, the commander of the 2nd Battalion. Its turret markings were *II 01*, augmented by a black, white and red pennant on the antenna. The crew are scanning the horizon for enemy movements.

German artillery, in this instance a *10-cm K18*, engages enemy tanks that have broken through.

A crew from the 4th Company observes the enemy from its *Panzer IV*.